Star-(
Guide to Hig
Lunar and Pla... ...maging

Dave Eagle
FRAS

STAR-GAZING
.co.uk

October 2022

Star-Gazing Astrophotography Guide
by Dave Eagle.

Welcome to my High Resolution Lunar and Planet Imaging volume of my astrophotography guides.

My guides cover many techniques developed over the years and originally stem from my very successful hands-on astrophotography workshops. These workshops cover many aspects of astronomy, astrophotography, high resolution planet and Moon imaging as well as image processing.

The techniques and workflows shown here should be help the newcomer to understand how best use of the software to become more proficient at achieving better results when using high speed cameras to capture both Moon and planet images.

The methods outlined in these pages is certainly not the only way to do things. The workflows that follow in this guide are certainly the simplest way I have found to achieve fantastic results when capturing and processing my Moon and planet images.

I hope that you find this guide useful.

If you have, look out for some of my other astrophotography guides and upcoming workshops.

Astrophotography Guides:
www.star-gazing.co.uk/WebPage/astrophotography-guides

Workshops:
www.star-gazing.co.uk/Workshops.html

Dave Eagle FRAS.
www.star-gazing.co.uk

Star-gazing Guide to High Resolution Lunar and Planet Imaging

Table of Contents

High Resolution Lunar and Planet Imaging.......... 5

The Inner Planets.......... 6

Mercury & Venus.......... 6

The Outer Planets.......... 10

Mars.......... 12

Jupiter.......... 15

Saturn.......... 16

Uranus & Neptune.......... 18

Pluto.......... 19

The Moon.......... 19

The Sun.......... 21

Capturing Images.......... 21

Imaging Setup.......... 21

Telescope and Focal Length.......... 21

Collimation.......... 22

Cameras.......... 22

Camera Pixel Size.......... 22

Mono Vs One-Shot Colour.......... 23

Producing Colour images.......... 23

Accessories.......... 25

The Atmospheric Dispersion Corrector (ADC).......... 25

Barlow Lens.......... 27

Extension Tube.......... 27

Focal reducer.......... 28

Filters.......... 28

Capture Software.......... 29

Capturing Images in SharpCap.......... 29

Capturing videos using SharpCap.......... 32

Image capture settings. 32

Tracking. 36

Focusing. 36

Processing The Captured Videos. 38

Stacking using AutoStakkert! 39

Stacking using AstroSurface. 49

Post-Stacking Image Processing 56

Registax RGB Alignment. 56

Registax Colour Balancing. 58

Registax Wavelet Sharpening. 60

AstroSurface Sharpening. 63

AstroSurface White Balancing. 67

Final Image Polishing. 68

Post processing using Photoshop. 68

Rotating and cropping images. 68

Brightness Adjustments. 69

Sharpening The Image. 70

Increasing Colour Saturation. 71

Revealing fainter detail. 72

Post Processing using Affinity Photo. 75

Rotating and cropping images. 75

Brightness Adjustments. 76

Sharpening The Image. 76

Increasing Colour Saturation. 77

Revealing fainter detail. 78

Other Useful Software / References 82

High Resolution Lunar and Planet Imaging.

A WARNING! Before we start, there is something that you should be aware of before we start. Imaging planets can be challenging.

To get a decent sized disk size for imaging, very high magnifications are required. As well as magnifying the image, this shows up optical errors, turbulent seeing, atmospheric dispersion and tracking problems.

This guide outlines many of the techniques and workflows that I use to capture and process Moon and planet images. It has been written to help you get started in using these techniques to get the best out of your moon and planet images.

I always try to use the **KISS** Method with all my image processing.

Keeping **I**t **S**tupidly **S**imple.

I hope that my guide helps you keep it as simple as possible and get going to produce some very nice Moon and planet images.

High resolution imaging is almost like magic, managing to draw out intricate detail, even when the seeing looks absolutely appalling. Some people even call it Lucky Imaging.

The technique relies on the camera taking of lots of individual images very quickly by capturing a video. The video and its stream of images captured in frames are scanned using specialised stacking software, analysed, and sorted by quality. The most blurred images are rejected, the sharpest images retained and stacked to produce a single combined image. During this process, noise, being random in each image, smooths out and can almost disappear.

Any real features captured add up, so start to stand out in greater detail in the final stacked image.

The circumstances of the planets and The Moon are all different, which affects how they can be captured and what can be seen. This section of the guide gives an overview of the behaviour of the planets and Moon, as well as what to look for and features that can be captured.

The Inner Planets

Mercury & Venus

These two planets orbit closer to The Sun inside Earth's orbit, so are known as the inner (inferior) planets. They move faster in their orbits and their motion across the sky is much quicker than any other planet. Added to this, they do not venture that far from The Sun. Venus reaching as far as 47°, Mercury no more than 28.3°.

As they move from around The Sun, they are seen alternatively on each side of The Sun, reaching their maximum elongation, either east or west. When on the eastern side, they are visible in the western sky after sunset. On the western side, visible in the eastern morning sky before sunrise.

Not all apparitions are favourable for viewing. Their visibility depends on the angle of the ecliptic in the sky at the time of elongation. This angle, which changes throughout the year, dictates if an elongation coincides with a favourable tilt keeping the planet high in the sky before sunrise or after sunset. As a rule of thumb, from the northern hemisphere, eastern elongations (evening apparitions object in the western sky) are more favourable between February and June. Western elongations (morning apparitions in the eastern sky) are best seen between September and November. It is the opposite way round in the southern hemisphere.

Under favourable conditions, Venus can rise over 5½ hours before The Sun, or set 5½ hours after Sunset, so it can be viewed against a reasonably dark sky. Mercury, by contrast, stays very close to The Sun, only seen in a twilit sky, making it very difficult to observe and image.

Mercury also moves so fast, so it will not linger in a favourable position for very long, usually less than 10 days, before fleeing back into the Sun's glare. This makes it very easy to miss an apparition, especially if there is a run of cloudy skies (again!).

As well as Eastern and Western elongation already discussed, the planets can be at inferior and superior conjunction. These points are reached when the planet is almost lined up directly with The Sun and Earth. Inferior conjunction when it is almost between The Sun and Earth. Superior conjunction occurring when the planet is on the other side of The Sun.

Being closer to The Sun dictates that the angle of sunlight as seen from Earth changes dramatically around their orbit, and like The Moon, both planets display phases as seen from Earth.

Due to the wide differences in the distances of the planets relative to Earth when they are located at different positions on their orbit, their apparent disk size as seen from Earth can vary enormously.

At superior conjunction, the planets display a full disk, but are extremely small, usually unobservable, located on the far side of The Sun. As they progress around their orbits, they emerge from the evening twilight, moving eastwards from The Sun becoming visible in the western sky after sunset. Moving further away from The Sun getting higher and higher in the evening sky each evening, they reach their greatest distance from The Sun. This is called eastern elongation. The planets apparent size has grown quite a bit since passing superior conjunction and displays a half phase. Passing eastern elongation, the planet now starts moving back towards The Sun, getting lower in the western evening twilight each evening. At that time, their apparent size swells even bigger as the distance from Earth decreases, now sporting a very nice crescent phase. Their disks get bigger, the phase becoming thinner as they approach The Sun, soon to lost in the evening twilight. At inferior conjunction, the planets are now at their largest apparent sizes, but the night side is turned towards Earth.

They are usually too close to The Sun to be seen when at inferior conjunction. Venus may be spotted as an extremely thin crescent a few degrees away from the Sun when at inferior conjunction, but this should not be attempted unless proper precautions are taken. The atmosphere backscatters IR and UV light from The Sun, so can damage eyesight or equipment.

Venus imaged approaching and passing inferior conjunction taken during the day, showing the changes in apparent size and phase. April to June 2020

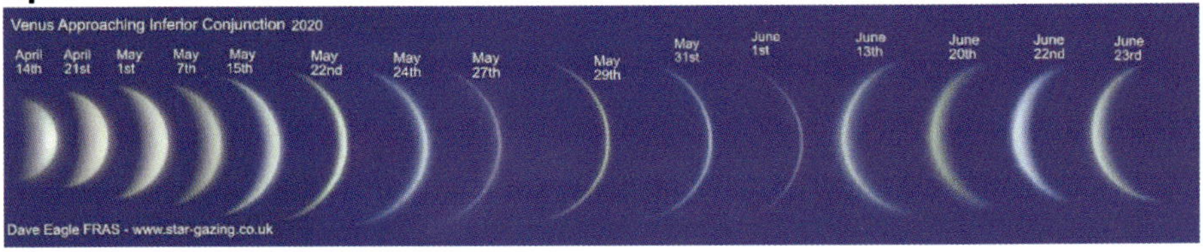

Occasionally, if the alignment of the Earth, Planet and Sun is right as it passes between The Earth and Sun the planet may be seen transiting across the face of The Sun. These transits are extremely rare, especially for Venus.

The next transit of Mercury is in November 2032, the last one being in November 2019.
Venus was last seen transiting The Sun in 2012, the next one visible from Earth is in December 2117.

After inferior conjunction, the planets move out of the Sun's glare and start to make an appearance low down in the eastern morning dawn. The planets apparent size shrinks as the distance from Earth increases. The phase also thickens as the planet moves away from The Sun. At their furthest from The Sun in the pre-dawn sky they reach western elongation, once again sporting a half phase. After this the planet starts losing altitude each morning, eventually disappearing into the morning twilight as they progress back towards superior conjunction, where the cycle starts all over again.

Mercury & Venus exhibit retrograde motion due to the orbital movement of Earth, but this is not quite as noticeable as the outer planets. Mercury always presents a real challenge because even at its furthest from The Sun, as it stays low to the horizon and is only visible in a twilit sky. Being about the same size as our Moon, it has no appreciable atmosphere. It has a solid surface covered with impact craters, but is incredibly difficult to capture.

Mercury imaged during the day showing just a hint of surface detail around the bright impact crater, Kuiper.

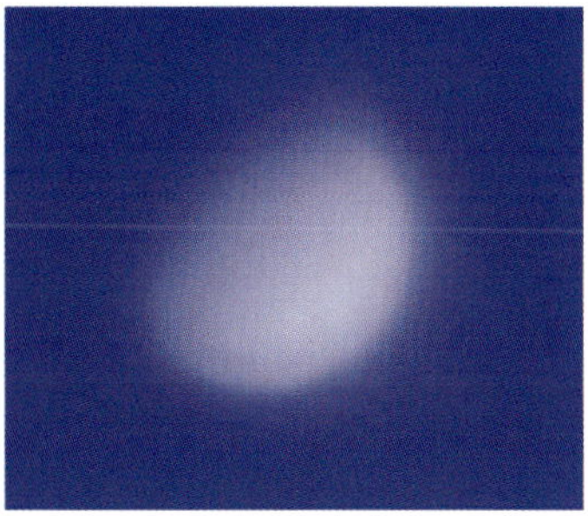

Venus, getting further from The Sun can be viewed in a darker sky, but is covered in a layer of thick white clouds. These reflect a lot of sunlight, making the planet extremely bright. This causes glare and light scattering within the telescope, smearing the image, making any subtle cloud features extremely difficult to see or capture. Because Venus is covered in this thick cloud layer, we are not able to see or image the surface.

Using the correct filters and a camera sensitive to infra-red light, surface features on the night side of Venus can be revealed through the clouds. This is a highly specialised technique and is not discussed in this guide.

Both Mercury and Venus can be imaged during the daytime if you know where to find them.

Of course, all safety precautions need to be made to prevent The Sun entering the telescope. Venus, at its brightest can often be seen with the naked eye during the day if known where to look safely.

The Outer Planets

The outer (so-called superior) planets, orbit further from The Sun than the Earth. As a result, their movements in the sky are completely differently to Mercury and Venus. The further a planet orbits from The Sun, the slower it moves along its orbit. Of the outer planets, Mars moves the fastest, Neptune the slowest. As they make progress along their orbit, outer planets appear to move west to east across the sky. This is known as their proper motion. Most planets move across the sky within a few degrees of the ecliptic, so are never too far away from this line.

The Earth, being closer to The Sun, moves faster than all the outer planets, so their visibility is primarily dictated by the movement of Earth around its orbit. When the planet is on the far side of their orbit from Earth on the other side of The Sun, they are at solar conjunction. The planet cannot be seen, as it is too close to the Sun in the sky at this time.

After passing solar conjunction, The Earth's motion causes it to start rising earlier than The Sun, emerging low in the morning eastern twilight just before sunrise. The planet rises earlier each morning, eventually reaching a point called western quadrature. This is where the angle between Earth, Sun and outer planet is at its greatest. Mars & Jupiter can exhibit gibbous phase at this position. This is also the time when any shadows of Saturn's disk on the rings is most pronounced.

As the Earth starts to overtake the outer planet its eastward (proper) motion against the background stars slows down, when seen against the background sky. The planet then starts to reverse direction, moving east – west which is known as retrograde motion. This is entirely due to the Earth's faster orbital motion as we overtake the planet
The planets rise earlier each morning, until they are up all night, rising as The Sun sets and setting as The Sun rises. It is now in the opposite

part of the sky from The Sun, reaching opposition. This is when the distance between The Earth and the planet are at their minimum. The best time to view it is around midnight, when the planet is at its highest in the southern sky and at its biggest apparent size and brightest.

As the planets orbits lie within a few degrees of the ecliptic, they move around the ecliptic and not all oppositions are the same. In the northern hemisphere, oppositions in the summer are very low down in our southern sky, so are less favourable. Northern winter oppositions are much more favourable as the planet is high up in the sky and well above the thickest part of the atmosphere in much steadier seeing.

After opposition, the distance from Earth increases, the planet starts slowing down, eventually becomes almost stationary again, before re-starting its original proper W–E motion across the sky. It has just finished performing a retrograde loop. The nearer the planet is to Earth, the bigger the retrograde loop.

The planet rises earlier and earlier each night, eventually becoming an evening object and setting before midnight.

It soon passes through a point called Eastern Quadrature. This is where the angle between Earth, Sun and outer planet is again at its greatest.

After this, the planet gets lower in the sky each evening, setting earlier each night, as it approaches and eventually slides into the evening twilight. It is now difficult to see and soon lost from view in The Sun's glare before moving back towards solar conjunction. Here the cycle starts again.

The outer planets can be imaged in the daytime, but the contrast is extremely low and can present a real challenge. Filters such as a 742nm or 807nm IR Pass ProPlanet Filter can be a useful tool for achieving this.

Mars

Unlike the other outer planets, which reach opposition every year, Mars moves so fast that it only comes to opposition once every two years or so. Not all oppositions are the same. The opposition in 2018 was very favourable, and it happened when Mars was at perihelion (closest to The Sun). This bought it a lot closer to Earth, so the apparent disk size was quite big. Perihelic oppositions of Mars occur when it is in the southern sky, so is quite low down as seen from northern latitudes. The 2020 opposition was in Pisces, so was a bit better for northern observers, but because it was a bit further away from Earth at that time, the disk was not quite as big as 2018, but was still quite large. Mars will not be seen from Earth as large again until 2033.

Apparent changing size of Mars captured during the 2020 apparition.

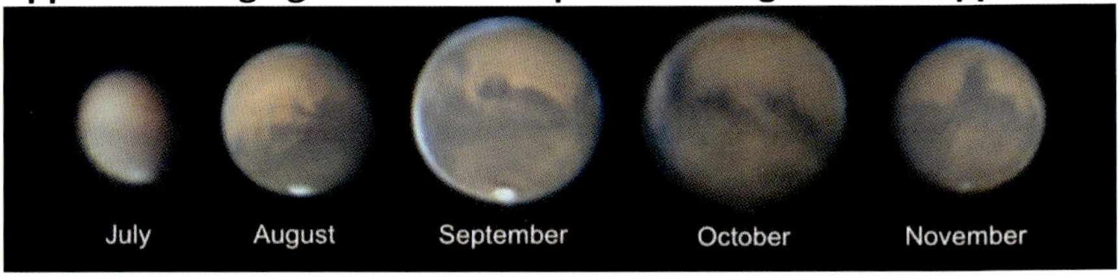

None of the other planets change in apparent size quite as dramatically as Mars. This is shown in the image below.

Maximum & Minimum sizes of the planets compared to The Moons limb as seen from Earth.

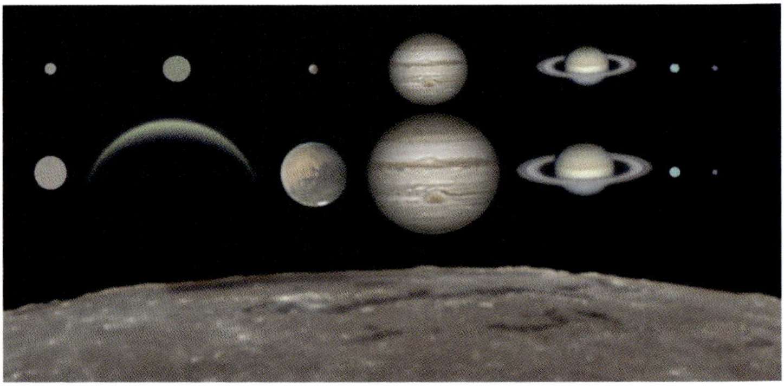

As with all the outer planets, Mars is best seen a few months either side of opposition, when it appears at its largest.
After opposition the distance from Earth increases its apparent disk size shrinks rapidly. When Mars is at its best, it is always advisable to make the most of any opportunity to observe or image it, as features soon shrink from view

Martian features to look out for.
Dark and light areas (areas of differing albedo). The most prominent are the dark triangular Syrtis Major and the bright Hellas Basin.

Many of these are named and are easy to identify using Mars maps or the BAA Mars mapper:
https://secure18.prositehosting.co.uk/secure_ssl/BAA/mars.html

Polar Caps. These can be seen to shrink as they are tilted towards The Sun and start to warm up during their Martian summer. This was very easy to see during the opposition of 2020.

The different faces of Mars. Images taken during the 2020 apparition. Note the size change in the south polar cap during Martian summer. (Not arranged in date order)

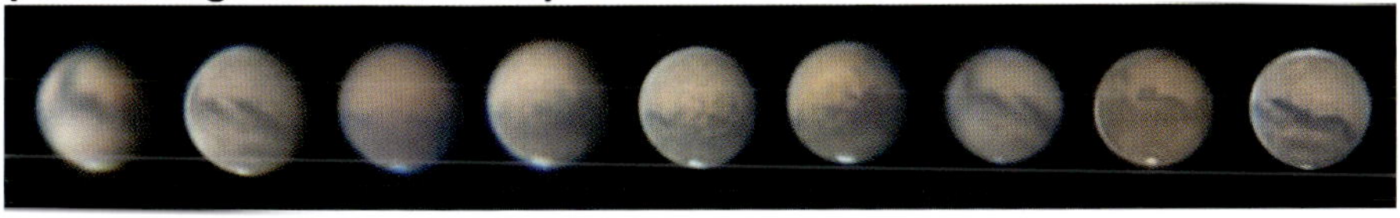

Clouds. These are most noticeable around the limb of the planet where they persist before and after sunrise/set on Mars. They can also often be seen over the volcanoes and often form hoods around both poles.

Vallis Marineris. This is a huge canyon that was discovered in 1972 by the Mariner 9 spacecraft.

Volcanoes. Mars has the largest volcanoes in our solar system. The three Tharsis volcanoes are a bit more of a challenge, but the enormous Olympus Mons, which would cover the whole of France, is visible as a bright spot on the surface.

Some prominent features on Mars.

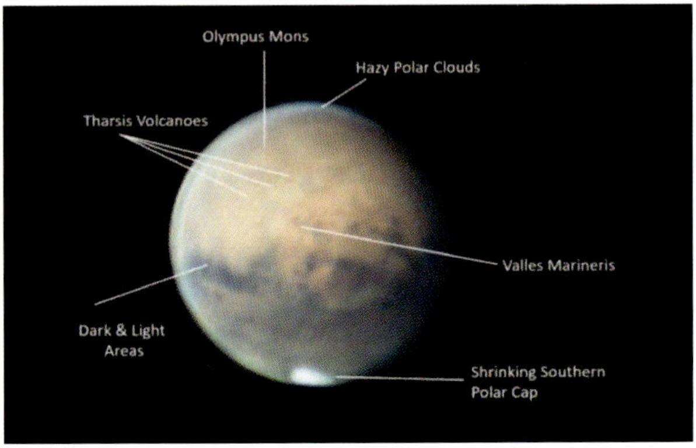

Dust Storms.

Mars has an annoying habit of having dust storms. The opposition of 2018 was spoilt by being cloaked by a dust storm which obscured many of the surface features while at opposition.

Mars has a rotation period of 24h 37m, not too dissimilar to Earths. This means that that at the same time on subsequent nights, the view we get of the disk is almost the same as the previous night. To catch a different face of Mars, it is required to go out at different times or wait until the feature you want rotates into view. Given that Mars is only at its best for a few weeks, make the most of any clear night and make long sessions of observing to get the best opportunities of seeing different features.

Mars has two moons, Phobos and Deimos. Being so small these are quite faint as seen from Earth, at magnitude +11 and +12 respectively at opposition, when Mars is at its brightest. That creates its own problems. The glare of Mars tends to swamp the moons, making them extremely difficult to observe and image.

Jupiter

This is the biggest planet in the solar system. Being so big, despite being so far away from Earth, its large size means details can be easily seen on the disk. Jupiter is the first and biggest of the gas giants. As a result, we are viewing the swirling tops of Jupiter's clouds.
Visible at first glance are the dark stripes across the disk. These are the cloud belts.

The dark stripes are known as belts, the lighter stripes, zones.

These belts and zones are named according to their latitude on Jupiter's disk.

Jupiter's Belts and Zones.

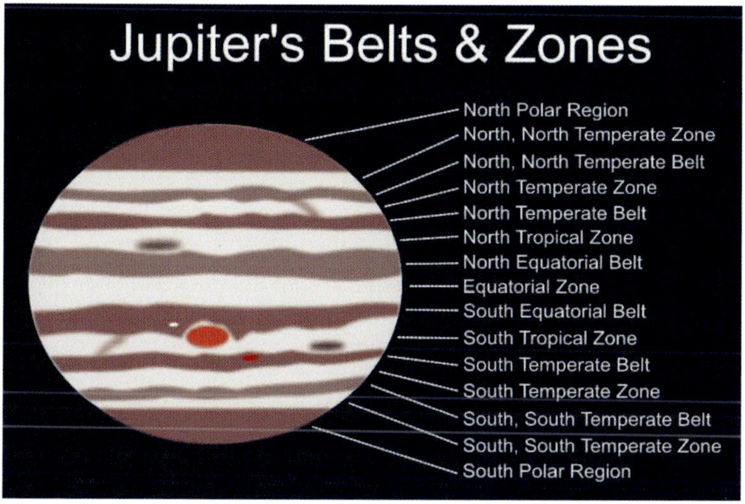

Being clouds, these are constantly in motion and changing. At times a dark belt can disappear and go missing for a period. There may be some hint of colour on the clouds visually, but high resolution imaging helps bring this out. The most colourful feature on Jupiter is the Great Red Spot. The spots colour has faded over the years, so not as red as it used to be.

The Red Spot is a swirling storm, almost twice the size of the Earth. It is not always seen as it is often on the other side of Jupiter's disk. It is clearly seen when it transits Jupiter's disk.

A list of the timing of the central Red Spot transits can be calculated using this Red Spot Transit Tool from Sky & Telescope: https://skyandtelescope.org/observing/interactive-sky-watching-tools/transit-times-of-jupiters-great-red-spot

Swirls, dark barges, bridges, festoons, and other smaller spots can be viewed within Jupiter's clouds.

The four Galilean Moons are also easy to capture. As well as seeing these moons on one side of Jupiter or the other, they can cause other interesting events. They often transit across Jupiter's disk, but as they are a similar brightness to Jupiter, can be hard to make out while in transit. The moons often cast shadows which also transit Jupiter's disk. These are a lot easier to see and capture, as they are so dark. The moons are extremely small, and they orbit Jupiter very quickly. To capture a sharp image of the moons or shadows, keep the length of the video captured below 40 seconds, otherwise the satellite or shadow blur due to their movement during the capture. Ganymede is so large it can be resolved by amateur imagers under excellent conditions.

When the angle is right, the Galilean moons also undergo numerous mutual events, passing in front of each other (occultation), or cast shadows on one another (eclipses). These are even more challenging to catch in detail.

Saturn

Saturn is the most beautiful planet in the solar system, with its wonderful ring system. Saturn's is a gas giant, the disk being very similar to Jupiter's with bands and zones running across the disk, named in the same manner. The atmosphere of Saturn has a high-level haze which makes these belts and zones much harder to see. Spots are also present in Saturn's atmosphere, but these can be difficult. Every few years a white spot appears in the atmosphere and can become very distinct.

The rings are made of a multitude of small particles covered in ice, orbiting around Saturn. The ring structure is challenging to catch.

The main two brightest rings are the most obvious. The outer A ring tends to be brighter than the inner B ring. These two rings are separated by a dark gap called the Cassini Division. This is a region where there are very few ring particles.

There is another much thinner gap towards the outer part of the A ring, called the Encke division, which is much harder to capture. Inside the B ring is the faint, tenuous and difficult to capture C, or crepe, ring.

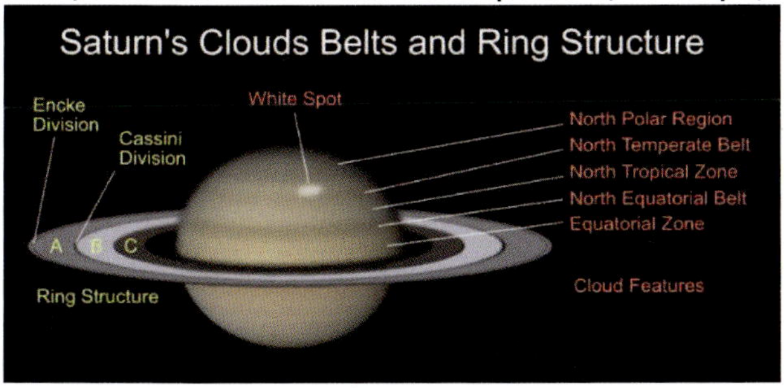

The aspect of Saturn's rings from Earth changes over the years, alternating between being wide open, very nicely displayed or edge-on and almost invisible. The divisions in the rings are a lot easier to capture around the extent of the rings, especially at their widest. When the rings are presented at a shallower angle, the divisions become more difficult.

The angle of presentation of the rings to Earth changes every 13 – 15 years. The next edge on presentation of Saturn's rings is in March 2025, being wide open again in 2032.

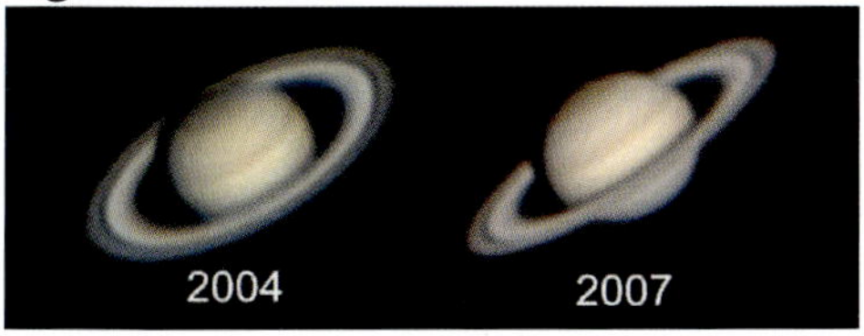

Saturn's rings are much brighter a couple of weeks either side of opposition. This is known as the Seeliger Effect.

Uranus & Neptune

These two ice giants are very big, but extremely remote way out in the outer solar system. As a result, their apparent disks are extremely small, and we are not able to see these very well. Uranus, which can just be brighter than +6th magnitude at opposition is just about bright enough to be seen with the naked eye. Neptune reaches about magnitude +8 so needs binoculars or a small telescope to identify it amongst the stars. The disks of both these planets are seen as small blue-green disks. The colour often giving them away. Capturing a small disk is relatively easy with Uranus, being a bit bigger than Uranus. Only very accomplished imagers with huge telescopes can capture an appreciable disk and details on the cloud tops. The Moons of these planets can also be captured if a longer exposure is used. Uranus' brightest satellite is Triton. Neptune has three moons bright enough for amateurs to image.

Monochrome Image of Uranus, Oberon and Umbriel and a colour image, just about showing the small bluey-green disk of Uranus.

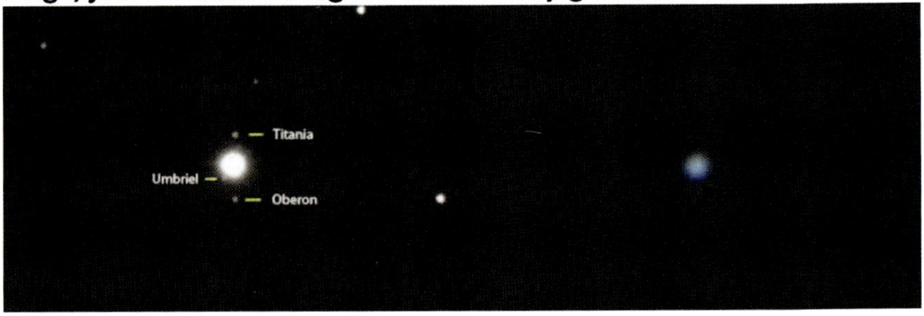

Monochrome Image of Neptune and Triton and a colour image. (Triton is the fainter object very close to Neptune).

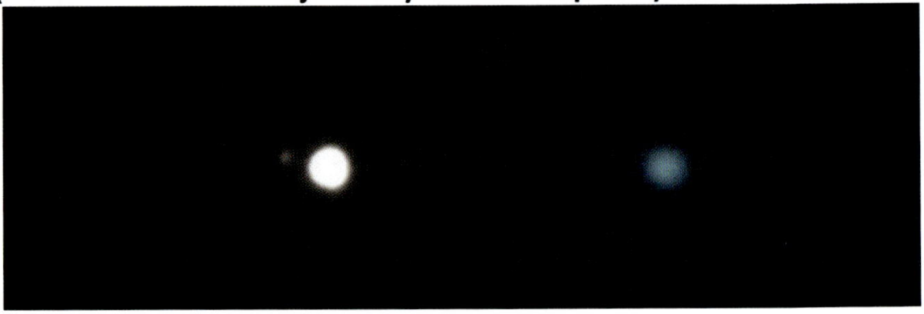

Pluto

Pluto, being just a small point of light, and extremely faint at about +14th magnitude, so is not suitable for discussing here as we are unable to capture it in high resolution.

The Moon

The Moon is the one celestial object that we can see in such fantastic detail. There is just so much to see at times, it is very easy to get lost amongst the jumble of craters splattered across its surface. The best part of the Moon to observe and image is the boundary between night and day, where The Sun is rising, or setting on the lunar surface. This is known as the terminator. It produces long stark shadows, making surface features really stand out and looking very dramatic. This moves across the disk as The Moon orbits the Earth causing the familiar changing phases. As The Moon draws away from the Sun just after New, it appears in the western sky after sunset, setting soon after the Sun. Each evening, the waxing Moon gets higher as the phase thickens, setting later each night as it moves eastwards, until it reaches first quarter when it sets around midnight. The phase thickens to gibbous and brightens as it approaches Full Moon.

At Full Moon it is opposite The Sun, rising at Sunset and setting at Sunrise. The phases are reversed after full when the waning Moon is visible in the morning sky.

Many different lunar features can be captured. These range from the dark, flatter maria, huge walled plains down to quite small craters and mountains. There are also several other features to look out for, such as rilles, crater chains, and lunar swirls, the most notable of these being Reina Gamma.

These features change in appearance hour to hour, depending on the angle of sunlight falling on them.

As the Moon orbits the Earth, it keeps the same side faced towards Earth, so we never see the far side.

The motion of The Moon in its orbit is extremely complex. As a result of the changes in orbital speed and its distance from Earth, this causes two effects called libration and nutation, which results in The Moon appearing to wobble. This allows us at times to see just around the limb so we can peer just a little bit further being able to glimpse features usually hidden from view.

A huge impact feature called Mare Orientale is located just over the western limb of The Moon. When libration is favourable for that side of the limb, we get a very nice view into the centre and the circle of mountains surrounding it. A fine sight indeed.

Other sights to look out for are Clair-Obscur effects. These are seemingly familiar shapes seen on the surface caused by the dark shadows and bright sunlight falling onto the surface features, usually close to the terminator. The most famous of these are the Lunar X and V, which are visible close to the first quarter phase.

The Lunar X.

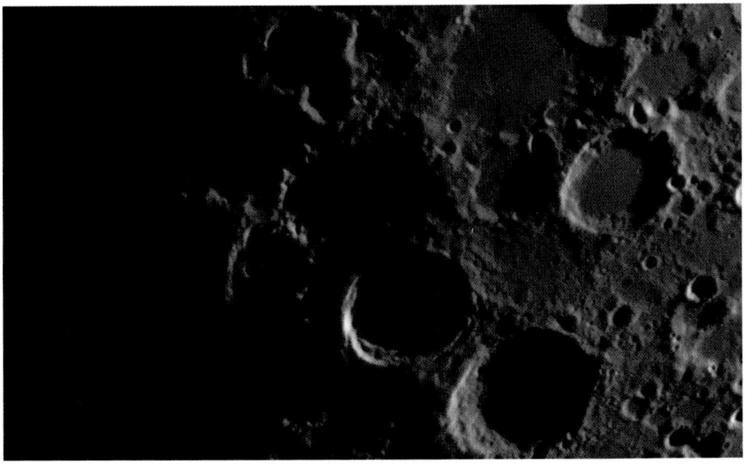

The Sun

The Sun is imaged using high resolution techniques. This really needs very careful filtering and imaging using a monochrome camera to capture the best results. As it is so specialised, solar imaging is covered in a separate guide. However, many of the post-processing techniques shown in this guide can be used for solar image processing.

Capturing Images.

Imaging Setup.

Telescope and Focal Length.

With all telescopes, aperture is everything. (Almost!). A larger aperture telescope gives a higher resolution. BUT! A larger resolution scope is also looking through a bigger column of air, so that it is more likely to be affected by atmospheric turbulence. A refractor is normally the preferred choice for observing and imaging the planets or Moon. These are prohibitively expensive over a certain aperture, so Schmidt Cassegrain Telescopes (SCT's) are the preferred choice these days, being a bit more affordable and having long focal lengths.

Depending on the objects being imaged, a different setup may be needed to get the framing required.

The field of view obtained depends on the focal length of the telescope and the size of the imaging chip in the camera.

A long focal length is crucial in getting the biggest scale image possible on the imaging chip, which is most desired for planetary imaging.
This is especially true for Mars, having such a small disk and lots of surface features to be captured.

If the whole disk of The Moon was required, then a telescope with a shorter focal length would be better. Depending on the scope used, the addition of a focal reducer can give an even wider field of view.

A telescope giving a narrower field of view can be used, but a series of overlapping images need to be taken to be stitched together in a mosaic to obtain the wider view.

A very useful Field of View Calculator is available at Astronomy Tools. Use it in imaging mode to show how large the planet or Moon disk appears in any telescope / camera / Barlow / reducer combination. https://astronomy.tools/calculators/field_of_view

Collimation.

When doing high resolution imaging of The Moon and planets, having an accurately collimated telescope is critical to produce the sharpest images. It is always good practice to ensure that the scope is well collimated performing high resolution imaging.

Cameras

There such a bewildering array of imaging cameras available these days, it is sometimes hard to tell which camera would be the best. A lot depends on the telescope being used and which type of imaging is being planned.

Cameras vary widely in sensitivity, BIT Depth, number and size of pixels, and exposure length range. These factors need to be considered when putting a planetary imaging rig together. A more sensitive camera requires a shorter exposure to produce a well exposed image. As a rule of thumb, the more sensitive it is and the shorter exposure the camera can take, it will be more expensive.

Camera Pixel Size.

This has a huge impact on the resolution of the images and the amount of detail captured in the images. A camera with bigger pixels has less resolution but usually more sensitive to light. A camera needs to be matched to the telescope it will be used with.

There is no point in getting a camera with very small pixels to achieve a very high resolution if the scope is not able to give an image at that detail. In this case it results in over-sampling.

The opposite is using a camera with large pixels on a scope which gives a higher resolution. This results in under-sampling.

Astronomy Tools CCD Suitability Calculator can be used to match a camera to a scope: http://astronomy.tools/calculators/ccd_suitability

To calculate the resolution of any telescope / camera combination, divide the pixel size by the scope's focal length, then multiply by 206.3. This gives you the resolution in arcseconds per pixel ("/pixel).

In high resolution imaging we are trying to achieve the smallest possible resolution value.

Mono Vs One-Shot Colour

Producing Colour images.

Most people are surprised to hear that no colour is detected by a camera chip. Cameras, even one-shot colour ones, have chips which produce a monochrome image.

To produce a colour image, each pixel needs to infer some colour information. This is achieved by placing a coloured filter on top of the imaging chip. With a monochrome camera, individual filters can be used independently for Red Green and Blue (RGB) imaging. In this case three different images are taken using red, green, and blue filters in turn.

These images are then combined during post-processing to produce a colour image. This has its advantages as a mono camera is much more sensitive and of higher resolution as every pixel "sees" the colour data.

One-shot cameras have a layer of coloured filters built above the imaging chip, called the Bayer Matrix. This is designed so that a different colour filter sits above each pixel on the chip. This Bayer Matrix has three different filters: Red, green, and blue.
The software within the camera is programmed to know which pixel is underneath each colour filter, saving this information with the image.

This information can then be used by software, either within the camera, or by image processing software to produce a colour image.

A typical layout of a Bayer Matrix is shown below.

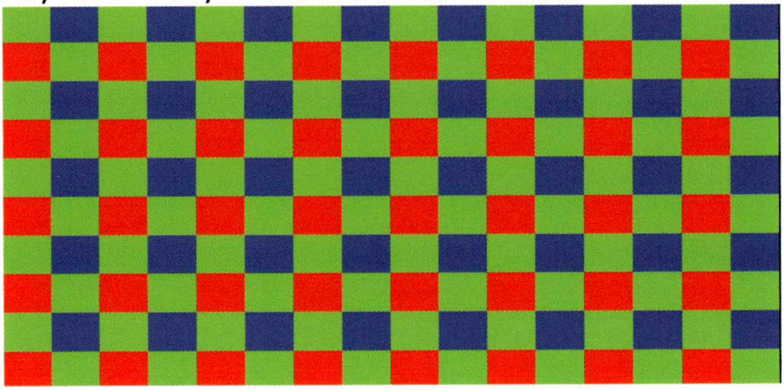

50% of the pixels have a green filter, 25% of them have a red or blue filters. The higher percentage of green filtered pixels can give a green tinge to some images.

When the Bayer Matrix is in place, if a blue filter lies above a pixel, only light near the blue end of the spectrum reaches it. The same goes for pixels under the red and green filters. This selective filtering stops quite a lot of light from reaching the imaging chip, as wavelengths away from the filters restrictive bandwidth never reach the pixel and photons are lost. Modern software is good in figuring out what should have been visible to those pixels but is just not the same as the chip receiving all the filtered light and capturing that data.

A one-shot colour camera is a lot less sensitive as less light reaches the imaging chip. As a result, the images are often darker, requiring longer exposures and the images are generally of lower resolution. The benefit of using a one-shot colour camera is that only one exposure is required to produce a colour image.

This is especially useful with Jupiter, which has a fast rotation period.

Accessories

The Atmospheric Dispersion Corrector (ADC)

Atmospheric dispersion occurs as a result light passing between medium of different densities. Atmospheric dispersion is caused by light passing into Earth's atmosphere from space. As light from a celestial object enters Earth's different wavelengths of light due are diffracted in slightly different directions to one another. The amount each colour is offset is dictated by its refractive index.

All wavelengths are affected to different degrees. Red light, being of longer wavelength, is less effected than light of shorter wavelength, like blue. This is the reason our sky is blue, and sunsets are red.

This results in each colour image being offset at a slightly different point, smearing the image, so it is not possible to get a properly focused image. Fine detail is lost in the resulting mess.

The ADC is used to correct this, bringing the wavelengths back together so that fine detail is once again possible to see and image.

Please note: The ADC can only correct atmospheric dispersion.
It cannot correct atmospheric disturbance, turbulence and seeing.

Seeing can be affected severely by the presence of a jet stream. If one is blowing overhead, this causes bad seeing, making it difficult to capture sharp images.

It's worth consulting the European Jet Stream Map here:
https://www.netweather.tv/charts-and-data/jetstream
Red areas show where the Jet Stream is active.

If trying to observe or image under a jet stream, the seeing is usually atrocious. On nights like that in those conditions, it might be best not to get set up and even try high resolution imaging.

The effect of atmospheric dispersion at different altitudes.

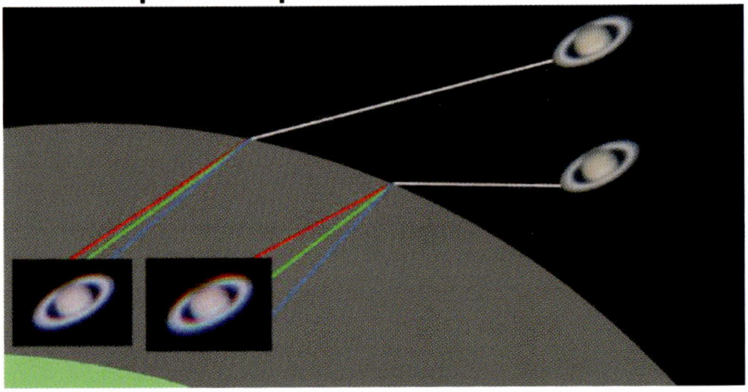

The lower the planet is in the sky, the greater the atmospheric dispersion and the worse the image is affected.

At its worse the different colour images are separated enough for red fringing to be seen at the top of the image with blue at the bottom.

An ADC has prisms which converge each wavelength back together. Once merged by the ADC, the image becomes a lot sharper, detail is much easier to discern, even when using a monochrome camera or when being viewed visually.
Some image capture software, such as SharpCap and ZWO's ASIStudio have an ADC Alignment Tool which helps to fine-tune the ADC to obtain the best correction possible.

The ADC Correcting Atmospheric Dispersion.

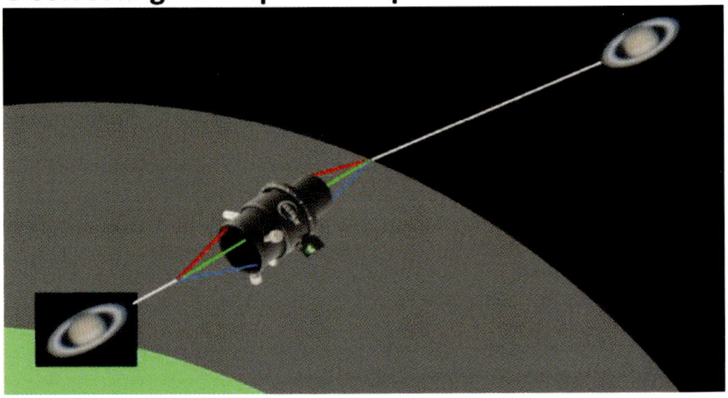

An ADC is an essential part of the planetary imager's artillery. It is really advised to use to help make images as sharp as possible, especially if the planet being imaged is low in the sky.

If the planet is high in the sky, the ADC may not be needed as the atmospheric dispersion is less of a problem.

Barlow Lens

A Barlow lens is placed between the telescope and camera to help achieve a bigger image of the planet on the camera chip.

A 2x Barlow effectively doubles the focal length of the telescope being used. The image of the planet produced by the telescope on the imaging chip doubles in size. Like most techniques this creates extra challenges. Adding any extra optical components into the light path potentially degrades the image. The light is also spread out a lot more, giving a darker image. Gain or exposure settings need to be increased to brighten the image when capturing. This can result in a slower frame rate and fewer individual images or more noise being saved to the video.

Extension Tube.

Adding an extension tube between the Barlow Lens and the camera an even bigger image of a planet can be made on the chip. By holding the camera further away from the Barlow lens, it increases the size of the image projected onto the camera chip. It's a bit like moving a projector away from a screen. As a result, the image produced is even bigger, but also a lot fainter. This increases the problems in trying to obtain a well exposed image and a high frame rate.

Please note that, although providing similar enlargement to an image, the 2x, 2.5x and 4x Powermates do not have the same projection effect to enlarge the image like a Barlow. As a result, an extension tube is not very effective in enlarging the image when used with these models.

Focal reducer.

These can be used to obtain a wider field of view with a setup. This may be required to get a larger area of The Moon on the chip, or, more rarely, to capture two planets close together so they are in the same field of view. Focal reducers are often specifically designed to fit a particular scope. A more cost-effective 1.25" focal reducer can be purchased which fits directly into the nosepiece of the camera.

Filters

UV/IR Cut filter. Although we cannot see it visually, many cameras are sensitive to UV and IR light. This comes to a different focal point in our imaging setup and tends to smear and blur the image. UV/IR Cut filter removes these wavelengths. If using a one-shot colour camera this is an essential part of the setup. The filter can be screwed into the 1.25" nosepiece of the camera.

UV/IR Filter fitted in 12.5" camera nosepiece.

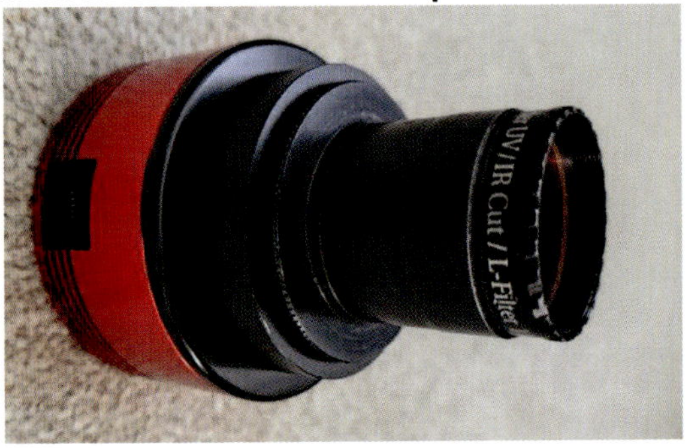

Coloured Filters. There are many coloured filters available these days, but am only going to mention the most used. A red filter can be used to enhance surface features on Mars or darken a daylight sky to image Venus & Mercury during the day. A yellow filter is useful for surface features of Mercury in daylight as well as cloud belts on Jupiter and Saturn. An orange filter can be used with Jupiter and Saturn to reveal cloud belt details. A red or Ha filter are useful for imaging The Moon with a monochrome camera, which really helps to steady seeing in an unsettled atmosphere.

Capture Software

Many cameras come with their own image capturing software. For example, ZWO has its own ASIStudio, but can only be used with ZWO cameras. Several free image capture software packages are available, which can be used with many different makes of camera. These are listed at the end of the guide.

Capturing Images in SharpCap

www.sharpcap.co.uk

This software is freely available. There is a paid licensed version which gives access to several other useful features.

As this can be used with most cameras, the demonstrations shown in this guide are performed with SharpCap.

SharpCap needs a few settings changed before starting.

From the menu, click **File > SharpCap Settings**.

Click the **Filenames** Tab and select the folder where the images are to be saved.

Under **Dates and time**, make sure that the following boxes are ticked.

Use UTC times in file and folder names.

Use Sortable date format (YYYY-MM-DD).

Create WinJUPOS Compatible File Names.

This naming method helps with sorting and finding the files later, as well as providing information image times, capture and using WinJUPOS, if going on to use that later.

I do not usually tick **Create Subfolders for each sequence**, as I hate scrolling through lots of folders to find the images.

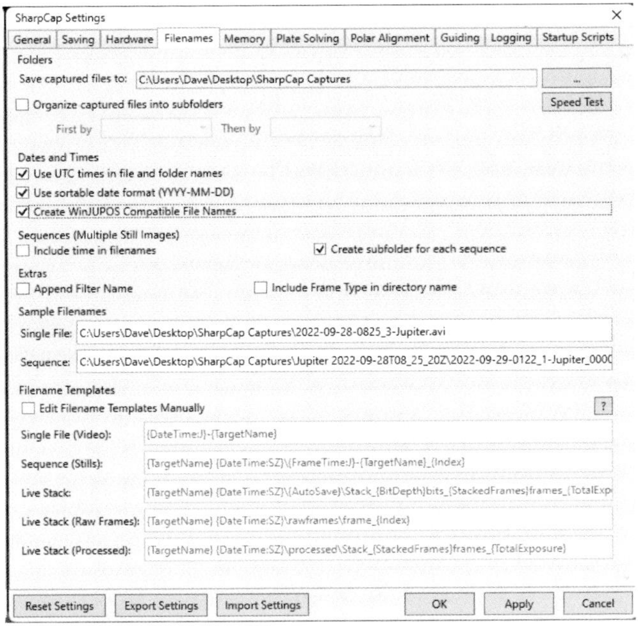

Click **Apply**, then **OK**.

Plug the camera into the USB port.

From the menu click **Cameras.**

From the dropdown menu, select the camera.

Once the camera is connected, a live view from the camera is displayed in the main window.

A menu with several options opens on the right hand side of the window.

This is where the camera settings are that will now need to be set up for successful capturing.

Capture Format and Area.

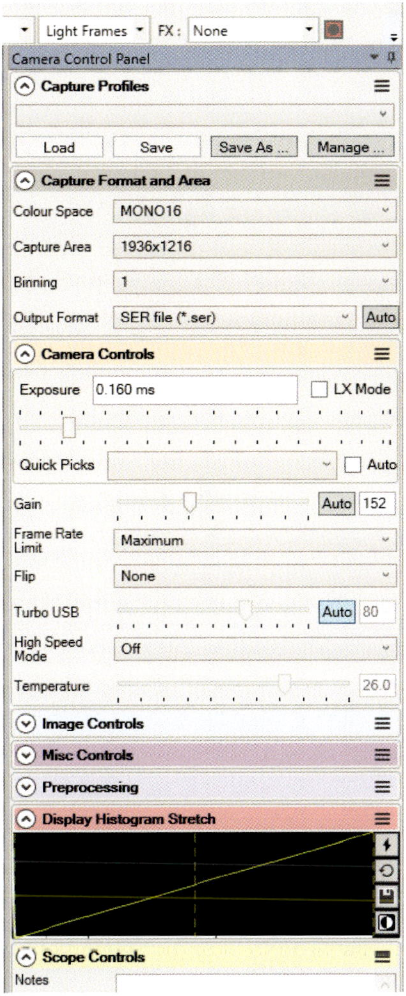

Colour Space. RAW8 or RAW16 are the BIT Colour Space settings for capturing raw data. RAW8 has less BIT depth than a RAW16, saving less data, producing smaller files.

Capture Area. This can be changed to use only part of the imaging chip to just capture a region of interest (**ROI**). This captures less blank sky making the images and video a lot smaller.

Binning. Leave at 1.

Output Format. AVI and SER video files. Raw8 saves AVI files, Raw16 SER files save more data. The SER videos are bigger, soon filling a hard disk.

Camera Controls.

Exposure. As short an exposure as possible is preferred to help to freeze any atmospheric disturbance which blur the image. Shorter exposures enable more individual frames to be captured in a set amount of time.

Gain. Gain is almost the equivalent of ISO in a DSLR. Turning up the gain multiplies the signal, making the image brighter if using a shorter exposure. This increases noise in the captured images.

Leave all the other settings as they are.

Now all is set to start capturing the video.

Capturing videos using SharpCap.

Image capture settings.

The exposure and the length of the video captured, as well as a few other factors, dictates how many individual frames are saved in the video.

The more frames that are captured, the better the resulting stacked image is (depending on the quality of those images, of course).

Exposure and Gain are the main settings used to obtain the best image brightness and fast frame rate. The settings used can change from night to night, or even minute to minute.

Once the planet or Moon has been centred in the field of view, adjust the exposure and gain settings to see the un-focused image of the planet on the screen. Refocus the scope, then re-adjust the exposure so that details are not washed out.
Getting a decent signal / noise ratio is important.

The exposure needs to be kept as short as possible with the gain kept as low as possible. Keeping both values too low produces a fainter image. If the image is too faint, there may not be enough data for the software to process. The resulting image is flat and lifeless or may not even process successfully. To ensure a bright enough image, exposure and / or gain need to be increased. Not having enough gain can produce an onion-ring artefact on planets.
Having too fast a frame rate can cause the camera to drop frames, which is not desirable as captured images could be lost.

The frame rate of capture depends on a variety of factors.

- The length of the exposure.
- The type of USB port used (USB2 or USB3).
- The quality and length of USB Cable used.
- The speed of a computer being used to capture the images.
- The speed of the computer hard disk.

Length of Capture / Frames Captured. The video can be captured using a length of video captured or a pre-determined number of frames. As a rule of thumb, the longer the duration of the capture, the more images are saved in the video. This gives more images for the processing software to stack. But the longer the video, the bigger the resulting file becomes.

Gamma settings can be used to help bring out different features, especially when imaging an object with a wide variation of contrast.
If imaging planets and the Gamma setting is available, this is usually set to 50. Some manufacturers have set and disabled the Gamma setting control in their cameras, so may not be available.

Image Control settings should be left at their default settings.
These do not affect the brightness of the data being collected, only how the image is viewed on the screen.
If set incorrectly, these can make the image look brighter or fainter than it really is. The histogram always displays the correct brightness of images being captured. Always refer to the histogram while capturing.

When adjusting Exposure and Gain settings, check the frame rate being captured bottom right of the SharpCap window, shown in frames per second (fps). In this case 14.5 fps.

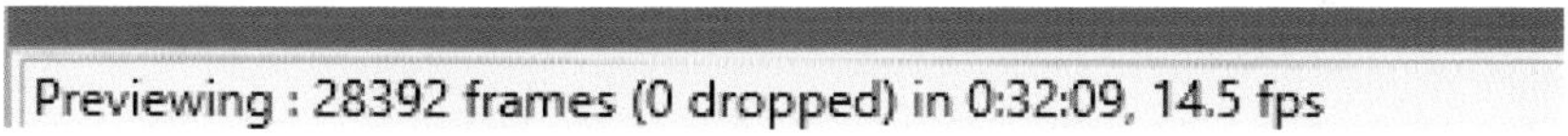

Aim for about 10 – 20 or more frames per second. Too low a frame rate results in not enough frames being captured to give a nice smooth stacked image, unless the video capture runs for longer. Having too fast a frame rate may result in frames being compressed to save them or even dropped and lost as the images cannot be saved fast enough.

To achieve the best result, it is always going to be a delicate balancing act between the two settings to get that crucial signal / noise ratio just right for that sessions conditions.

Adding a Barlow lens to increase the magnification spreads the light out even further, making the image fainter, resulting in these settings needing to be increased again resulting in the frame rate dropping. Very quickly it becomes evident just how challenging high resolution imaging can be.

Don't worry if the live image looks a bit grainy. Stacking the images smooths this out, if the data captured is good and many individual frames are captured and saved.

Whilst capturing, it is best to keep an eye the histogram to see what is happening to the light levels.
To see this open **Display Histogram Stretch** and check to see how far over to the right-hand side the graph stretches.

Settings and Histogram in SharpCap

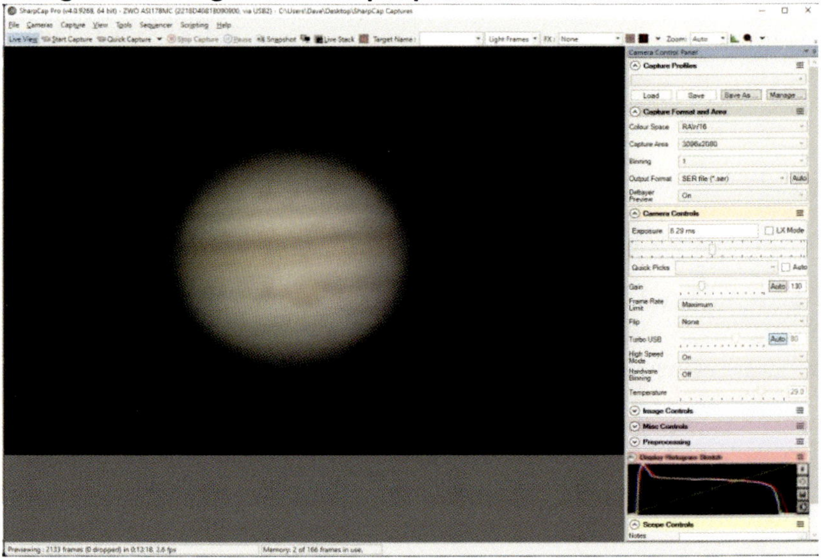

The histogram gives an indication of the distribution of pixels of different exposure, at a level of grey between the black point, on the left-hand side of the histogram, and the white point over on the right. The higher the line, the more pixels there are at that exposure.

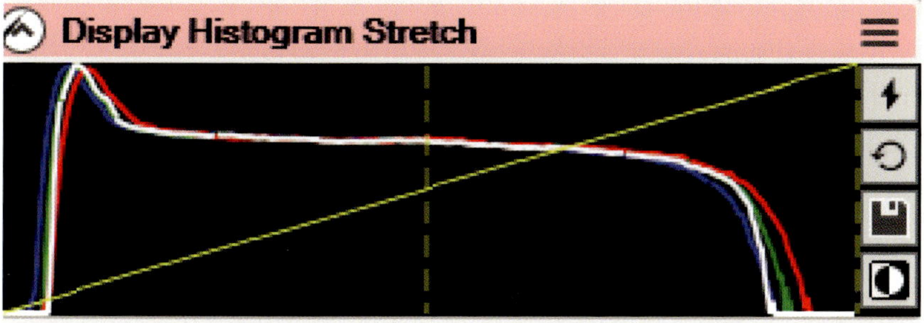

Try and adjust the exposure and gain settings so that right-hand side of the histogram curve almost, but not quite, touches the right-hand side of the scale. This ensures that the exposure is reasonably bright, but that no part of the image is over-exposed. This makes post processing easier.

If the lines on the right-hand side of the histogram is seen to start creeping down towards the left, it means that the brightness is fading during the capture. Something may be cutting off the amount of light reaching the camera.

If so, check that the telescopes front corrector plate or lens isn't starting to collect dew as the scope cooled down, thin clouds haven't gone across the object being imaged, or the object is going behind a tree or other obstruction. These darken as well as blur the image.

A misted corrector plate or lens can be resolved by blowing warm air gently over the surface using a hair dryer or using a dew heater.

Don't warm it up too much, as this could affect focus, or produce unwanted air currents and distort the image.

Tracking.

Unlike deep sky imaging, accurate tracking is not quite as important. It is OK to have the planet or Moon slowly drift across the field of view which capturing the video. When taking images of the planets, I often set the mount to Lunar tracking.

When imaging The Moon, I often use Sidereal tracking. This results in the image slowly drifting across the field of view while being captured. The reasons for doing this is revealed when we come to the processing steps later.

Focusing.

Capturing high resolution images is extremely sensitive to atmospheric changes and temperature. As a result, the point of focus can change constantly. It is good to keep on top of this, even adjusting focus when a video is being captured to maximise the number of sharp images taken. An electric focuser helps with this as focus can be adjusted without touching the telescope, shaking the image, and avoiding the effect of mirror flop in some SCT's.

To start capturing a video, from the Menu, click the V just to the right of **Quick Capture**.

From here the number of frames, or time length of the video can be selected.

Set the capture length needed to capture enough individual frames for stacking. Stick with about 60 second captures, although longer videos can be captured of Saturn, Mars, Uranus & Neptune which rotate slower, allowing longer videos to be captured without blurring.

If the frame rate is too fast for the computer and cannot be saved or put into buffer, images may be dropped and lost. Watch out for this.

The aim is to get a nicely exposed image and as fast a frame rate as possible, without dropping frames.

When capturing lunar images, the area closer to the terminator is darker than the rest of The Moon. This needs to be taken into consideration when setting the exposure, especially if taking several overlapping images to stitch together to create a bigger mosaic.

If imaging Jupiter and Galilean moons, do not capture for more than 40 seconds, which helps to freeze their rapid rotation and movement. Even a 60 second exposure can make Io elongate in the stacked image.

Once clicked, the video capture starts automatically.

Don't worry if the colour is seen to change as the video is captured. The stacked image averages this out, plus the stacked image can also be colour corrected.

Depending on the size of the planet, the size of the captured image can be changed by reducing the resolution of the camera, using an ROI. Doing this, captures less empty space around the planet significantly reducing the size of the images and frame rate will increase. The smaller field of view gives the extra challenge of keeping the object centred, especially if the mount is not accurately polar aligned. If the planet drifts towards the edge of the ROI, SharpCap has **Tilt** and **Pan** buttons which can be used to manually adjust the position of the ROI on the chip while the images are being captured. This helps to keep the planet in the centre of the field of view during the capture.

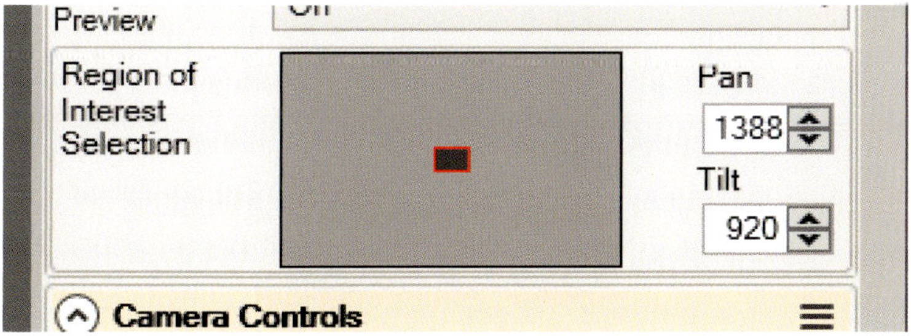

FireCapture also has built-in image stabilisation while capturing but I have not explored this.

If the video capture needs to be stopped at any point, for example if clouds start interfering, click the **Stop Video** button.

Once the software has finished capturing, or stopped, the video is automatically saved onto the computer hard disk.

To capture another image with the same settings, click the **Quick Capture** Button. SharpCap remembers the last setting used.

When the capture finishes, if the frame rate has been very fast, there may be quite a number of images that haven't been able to be saved. These are stored into buffer. If this is the case, once the capture has finished, it could be a while before these have been successfully saved from the buffer into the video file before another capture can be started. An information prompt pops up if this is the case.

Processing The Captured Videos.

There are a few pieces of software available for processing the captured videos. Traditionally, Registax was my preferred choice, before switching to AutoStakkert! After investigating more options for this guide, I have now moved over to AstroSurface for stacking videos. Both these software packages give better results than Registax. If capturing faint objects with a low signal / noise ratio, AutoStakkert! can have problems stacking the images. In these cases, I have found that Registax can often in many cases successfully stack the images, saving the data. Do not dismiss Registax completely.

All the images I have used for demonstration in this guide, as well as a few others, can be downloaded from my Web site for practice:
www.star-gazing.co.uk/HiResImaging

Registax.
This is free software. It can be downloaded from here:
http://www.astronomie.be/registax/download.html
Registax can be used to stack, but I have had some trouble with it not recognising a number of captured video files.

I have found AutoStakkert! and AstroSurface give better stacking results than Registax, so have concentrated on these two in this guide. Registax Stacking is not covered in this guide.

Stacking using AutoStakkert!

This is free software and can be downloaded here: https://www.autostakkert.com

When the software is opened, it comprises of two windows.
One is the **Control** window.
The other is the **Frame View** window.

AutoStakkert! Control Window

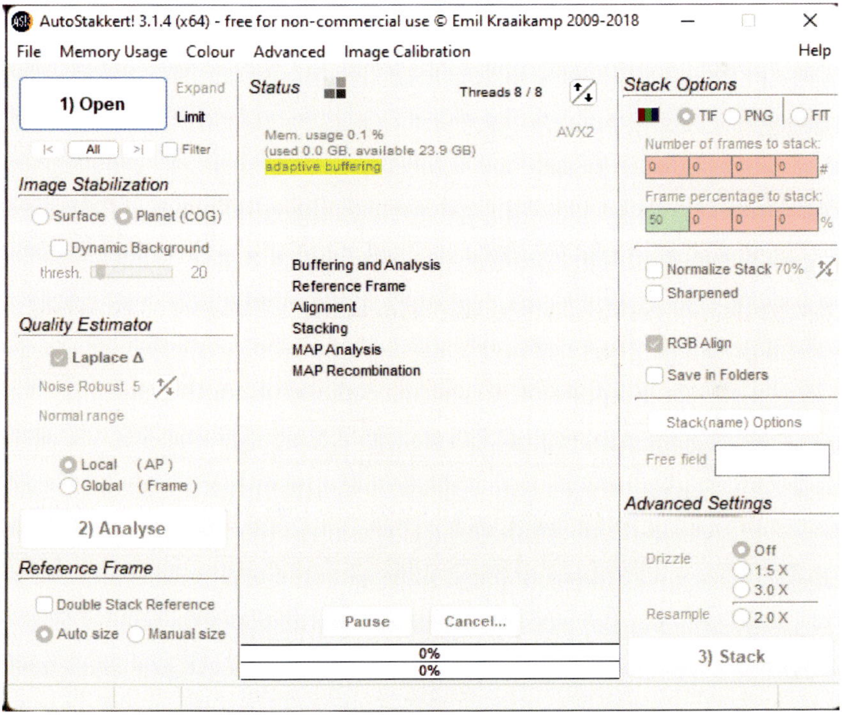

AutoStakkert! Frame View Window.

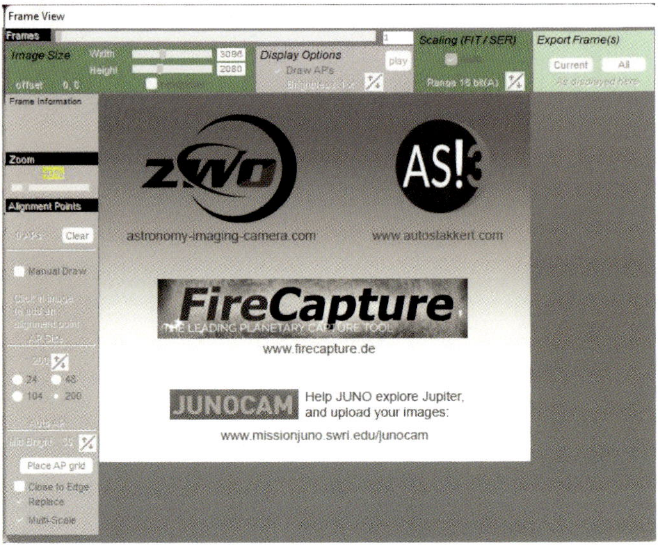

To open a captured video, press the **1) Open** button.

Browse to the folder where the video is saved and double-click on the video file to be processed.

The first frame of the video is displayed in the Frame View Window. The number of frames captured is shown **F#** NNNN/NNNN

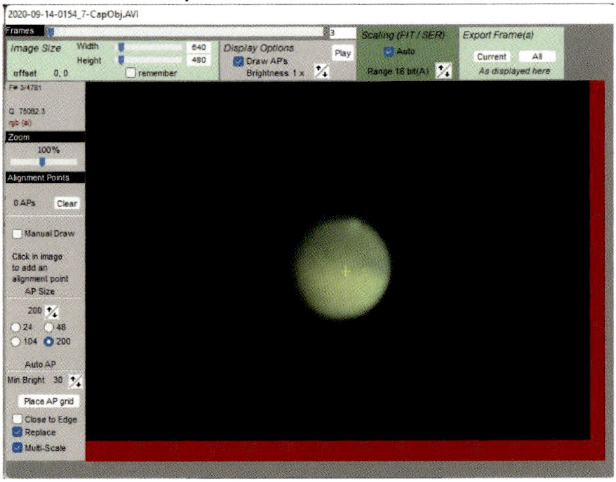

If the image is not fitting the screen, use the **Zoom** slider to adjust the view to suit. If the image is very faint, under **Display Options**, increase the **Brightness**. This will not affect the brightness of the images in the captured data, only how the images are displayed on the screen.

At the top of the Frame View Window is a **Frame**s slider. Moving this from side to side scans through and previews the captured frames where the quality of each image can be checked.

Under **Display Options**, the **Play** button can also be clicked to play the loaded video and **Stop** button to stop at a frame.

Before doing anything else, some changes need to be made to the settings in the Control Window, depending on the image being processed.
Underneath Image Stabilisation, select **Planet (COG)**, if processing a planet video. This setting usually displays a red border and nothing more needs to be done at this stage.

If processing a video of the lunar or solar surface, select **Surface**. When using Surface, there is be a slightly different view in the Frame View Window. An Image Stabilisation Anchor is placed on the image as shown below.

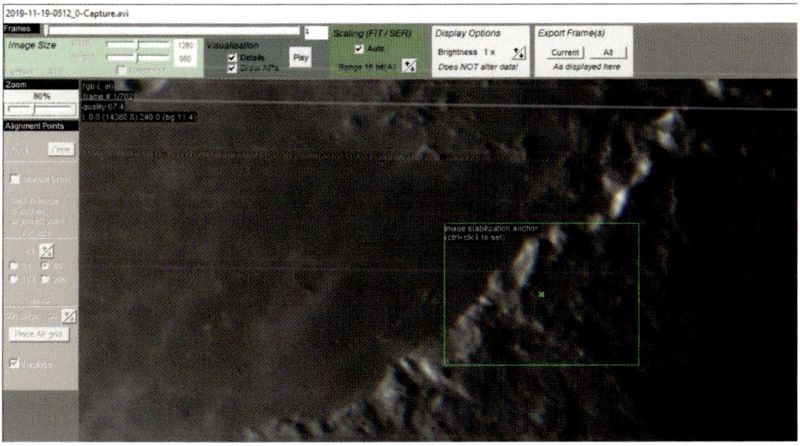

Hold down **Ctrl** and click an area where there is a lot of detail and plenty of different light gradients on the image, then click to place the Stabilisation Anchor. In the image above, a bright, detailed area along the Appenine Mountains was chosen.

If not happy with the position, this step can be repeated.

All is now ready to manage the settings in the Control Panel Window.

Start with the settings shown below.

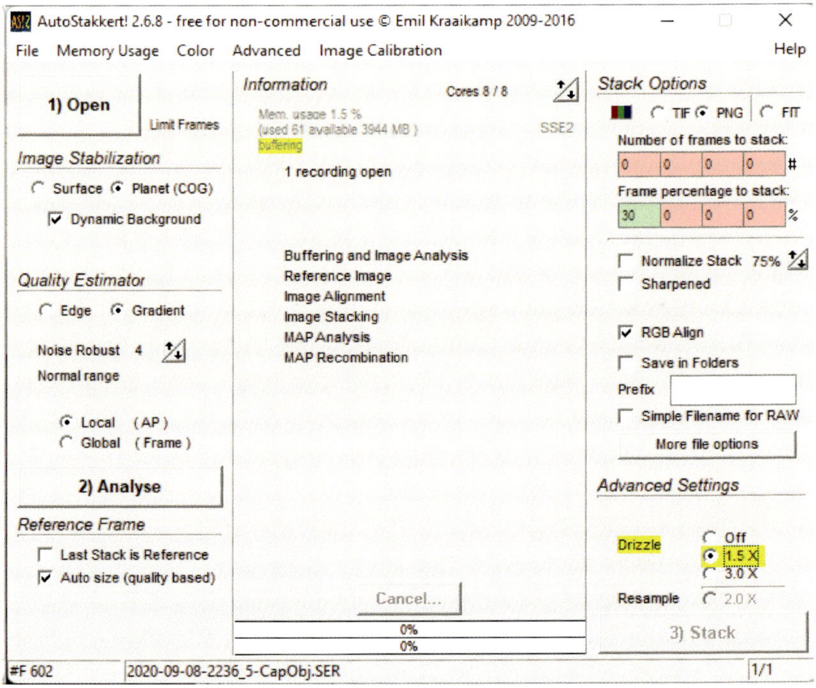

Use these as a starter, but feel free to adjust these as best suited for different video formats.

Under **Stack Options**, the **Number of frames to stack** in the video can be set.

Set the best 30% of the images captured under **Frame Percentage to Stack, saving** as a TIF or PNG file. If seeing is awful, reduce the percentage to something like 20% or even 10% on the very worse nights. A much higher percentage can be set when seeing is good.
Up to 4 different stacks can be set up.

Tick **RGB Aligned**.
Leave **Sharpened** unticked, as it sharpens the images just a bit too much. I prefer to do any sharpening later, using Registax, AstroSurface or during further post-processing, which gives a lot more control.
I do not like trawling through lots of sub-folders to find the final stacked images, hence my preference for not selecting **Saved in Folders.**

Under **Advanced Settings**, select a **Drizzle** Setting of **1.5 X** when possible. This is linked to the drifting of the image I mentioned earlier. I explain why I do this later.

When processing very large format video files, Drizzle may overload the software, running out of memory and freezing. Be aware of this issue when using a camera at full resolution and deselect it. If processing a video using a smaller imaging chip or **Region Of Interest (ROI)** this reduces the format and size of the captured video. The smaller files allow drizzle to be used without experiencing problems.

Once all the settings in the Control Window are as set up as required, click **2) Analyse**.

A couple of progress bars appear at the bottom of the window. When both reach 100% all the frames in the captured video have been analysed.

A green tick becomes visible beside **Buffering and Image Analysis**.

Below this is a graph showing the relative quality of the captured frames in the video.

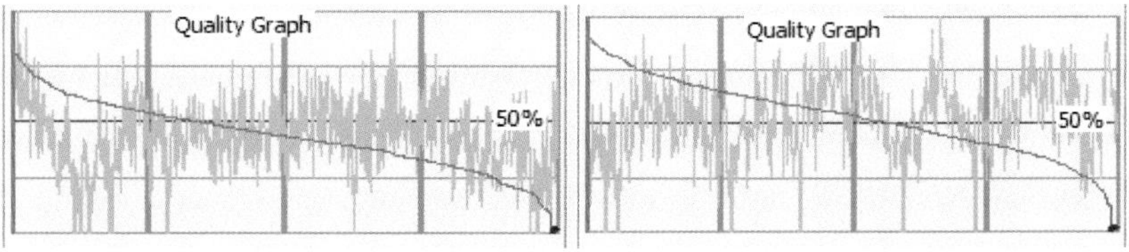

This graph can be used as a guide to inform you of the quality of the individual images in the captured video, to help make a judgement on how many or the percentage of images it is worth stacking for this video.

In the left-hand graph shown above, the quality of the captured images are not as good as the data shown in the right-hand quality graph.

Clicking the mouse within the graph displays the image captured at that point.

Any images below the horizontal 50% value, towards the right-hand side, are often not worth stacking. Their quality may be too low to add any value to the resulting stacked image and may even blur it.

From these graphs I would stack 30% of the images of the left-hand graph and 40% - 50% of the images for the right-hand one. If the seeing is well below par, I often reduce this to 20% or even lower. On a night with exceptional seeing, this can be increased to more than 50%. The aim is to stack as many images as possible to reduce noise and enhance features. The higher the number of good images that are stacked, the better the resulting image. If too many bad images are included in the stack, image quality suffers.

This takes a little bit longer to process and save the three different stacked images but is worth it to see which stack gives the best result, especially if trying this for the first time on the data.

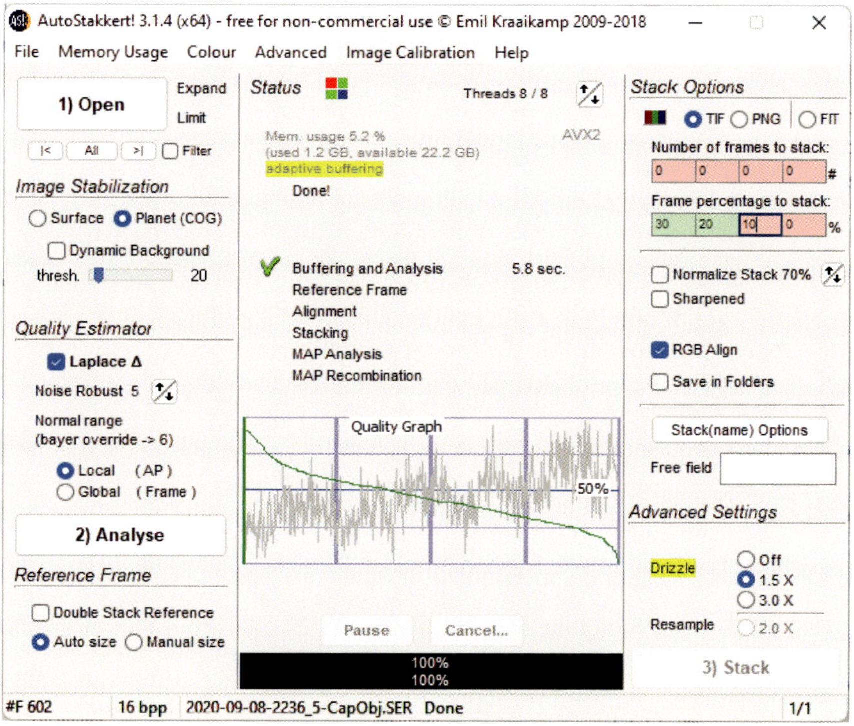

Go back to the Frame View Window. A red area may be visible in both Surface and Planet analysed images at this stage, around the edges, especially if the image was allowed to drift during the duration of the video capture.

Select an appropriate **Alignment Point (AP)** size for the image being processed as shown below.

Click the **Place AP grid** button.

Several overlapping squares appear over the planet or Moon image.

For smaller format videos and planets, I usually select an alignment size of 48, which gives me overlapping alignment points like those shown below.

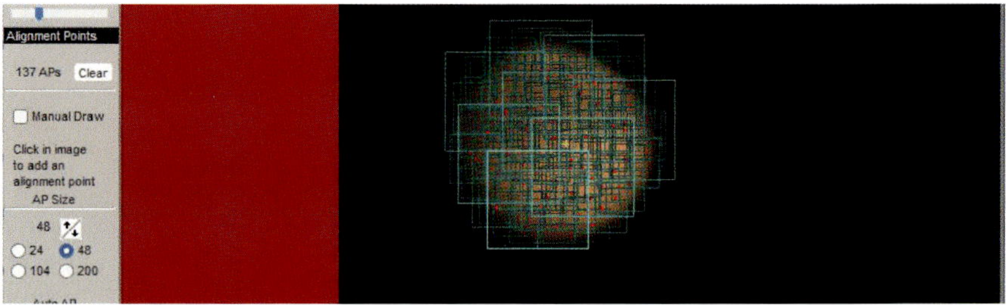

It is not recommend using the automatic placing of Alignment Points when processing planet images, but I have found that this works very well with most images.

Play around with all these settings to get the best result for the data.

For bigger format videos for lunar and solar surface images, I usually use an AP size of 104 or 200, which gives me something that below. Trial and error will identify the best settings to use best suited for the images captured.

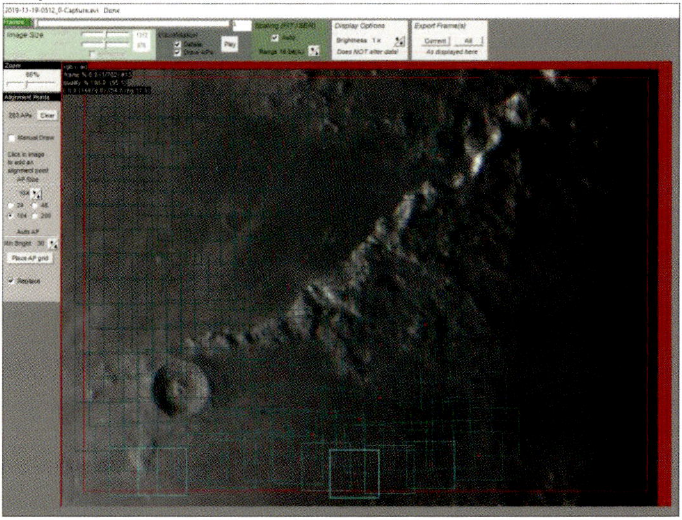

If too small an alignment point setting is used, the stacked image often shows a crazy paving style, which is certainly not ideal in achieving a great result.

Once the best size alignment points have been found for that data, this setting can be used consistently when processing.

If the planet or part of the Moon image is dark, especially near the terminator, it may not be completely covered with alignment points where detail can be seen. This can be seen in the image above. The lunar surface over on the right-hand side has detail visible but there are no automatically placed alignment points set onto it. This is because these pixels are darker than brightness limit set within the software.

This can be prevented by reducing the Minimum Brightness setting by clicking the down arrow on the **Min Bright** button. Click the **Place AP grid** button again to show the new AP grid. Keep adjusting the brightness and clicking the **Place AP** button until the required result is achieved.
Reducing the **Min Brightness** to 10, gave alignment points all the way across the into the darker area of the image for this video.

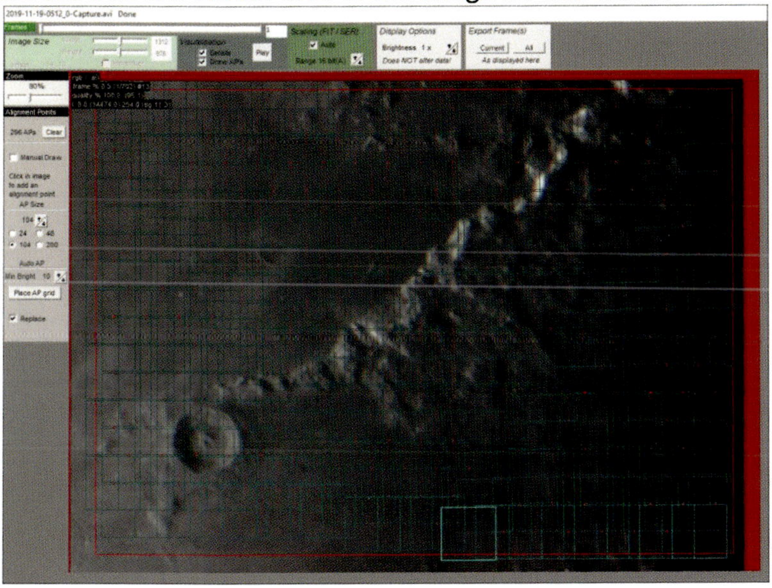

If needed, extra alignment points can be added by clicking on the image with the mouse.

When adding alignment points manually, make sure that they overlap with others to achieve the best result.

Once the alignment points are set, everything is ready to process the video frames to produce the final stacked image.

In the Control Panel Window, click the **3) Stack** button.
Two progress bars are seen progressing as the best images selected from the video are stacked.

Once the software has finished stacking, 6 green ticks are visible, with the times taken to do each step of the process.

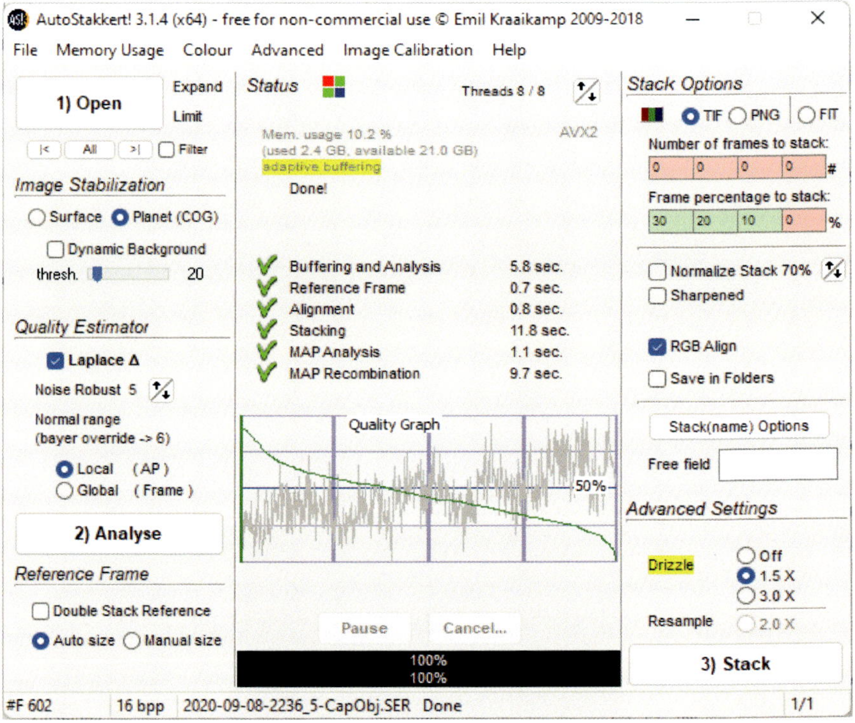

The software has taken the selected best images and stacked them to produce the final stacked images, which are automatically saved.

The stacked image is usually saved in the same folder as the video being processed. Occasionally, the software rather strangely saves the image in the parent folder above.

Check the image to see that has no stacking artefacts, which makes it impossible to get a good final image. If it has, try using a different alignment point size setting to see if that improves things. If not, then the images may just be too noisy and faint to stack correctly.

Check the dimensions of the resulting image. If the drizzle setting suggested has been used, the resulting image is bigger than the dimensions of the chip used to take the video. This is where our drifting of the image when capturing and drizzle helped us with a neat trick.

Any dust bunnies that may have been visible are smeared almost out of existence. The drizzle also enabled sub-pixel interpolation with a higher resolution to create a bigger image with a higher resolution than the camera chip. A total win-win!

Stacking using AstroSurface.

AstroSurface
http://astrosurface.com/pageuk.html
Free experimental Stacking and processing software.

Open AstroSurface.

From the menu.
Files > Open SER or AVI

Browse to the folder where the video file is stored and double-click on the file to open it.

When the video is loaded the Color Decoder Tool pops up.
The image appears blocky, noisy, and monochrome as shown below.

If a monochrome camera has been used, leave the setting on **1: Monochrome (or Raw ?).**

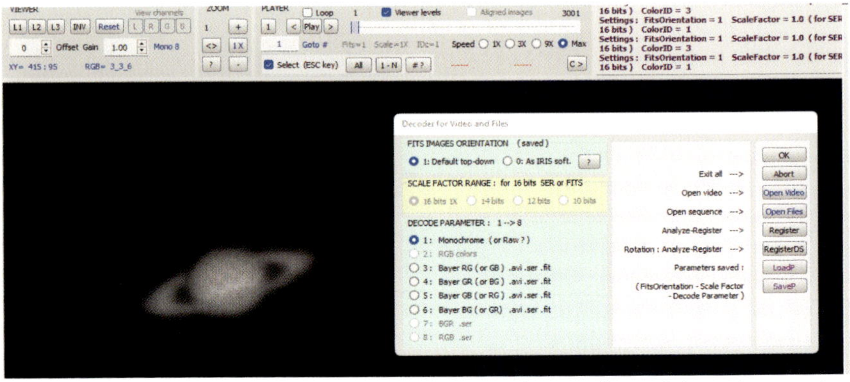

The area top right of the main window with purple writing shows the processes that have been carried out.

This video of Saturn was taken using a one-shot colour camera, so **3: Bayer RG SER or AVI raw** was selected. This debayers the image and retrieves the colour ready for the stacking process.

The individual image shown from within the video looks very grainy and pixelated as shown below.

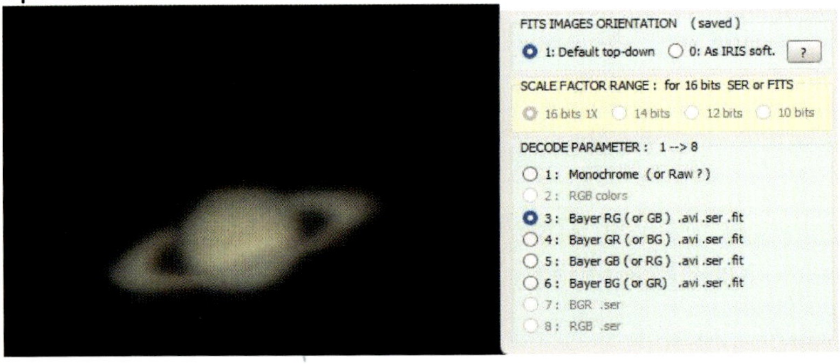

The combined image produced from the stacking process cleans and sharpens this up.

Click the **Register** button to open the **Analyse and Register t**ool.

Some of the options are greyed out and are not active until the previous necessary steps have been completed.

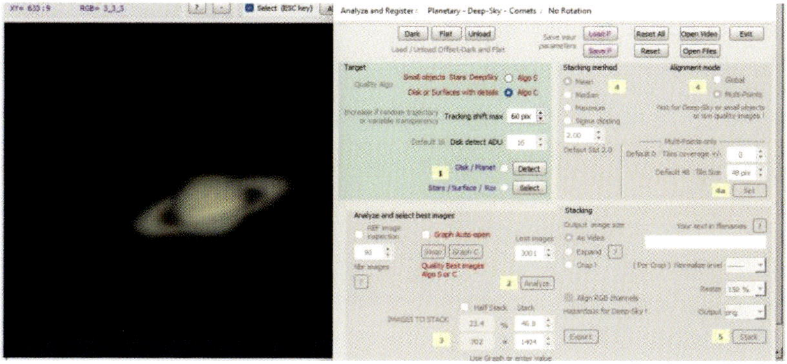

Follow the numbered prompts in AstroSurface to stack the captured frames.

1. Target.

For both planet and Moon videos, select **Disk or Surfaces with details – Algol C.**

For processing planet disk videos by **Disk / Planet** click the **Detect** button.

A yellow box appears around the planet.

Double click within the box to select it and a couple of green shaded boxes appear around the planet.

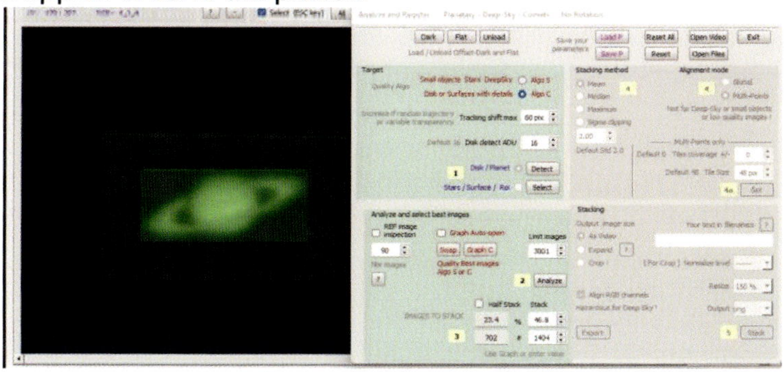

For processing Moon and solar images, beside **Select** by **Stars / Surface / Roi**, click the **Select** button. Use the mouse to draw a box around a part of the image that has lots of contrast and nice details.

If the box turns Red, the box is either too big, there's not enough detail in the image, or the selected region is too dark or bright.

If the boxes stay green, all is well and good.

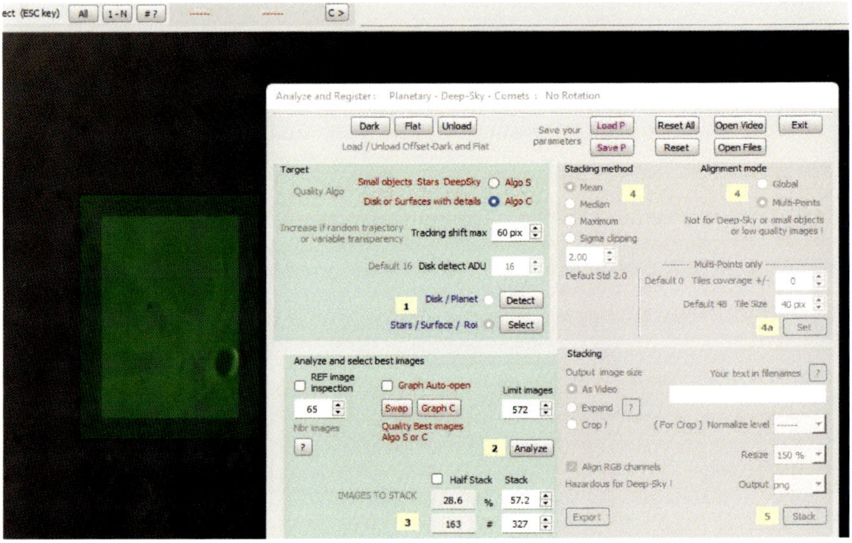

2. Analyse and select best images.
Put a tick in **Graph Auto-open**.

Click **Analyse.** A yellow progress bar appears.

Once all the images in the video have been analysed, the quality graph opens.

If **Graph Auto-Open** isn't ticked and no quality graph pops up, click the **Graph S** button.

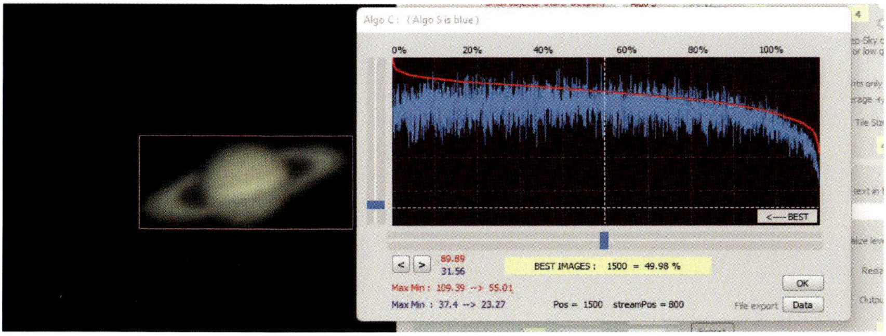

The graph displays the best images on the left hand side, the worse images on the right.

This graph shows the best number of images or % value to use to include the best images in the video to create the stack.
In this case it states there are 1500 best images = 49.98%.

The slider on the graph can be moved to left or right to include less or more of the captured images in the final stacked image.

Click **OK** and the displayed value are applied into **3. IMAGES TO STACK.**

Compare the quality graph above with the one below from a Mars video that was taken in less-than-ideal conditions.
Thin cloud started to interfere almost halfway through the capture and had to stop capturing as cloud increased, resulting in less captured images.
The sharp drop off in quality can be clearly seen just after 40% and there are a lot less "**BEST IMAGES**" at only 5.5%.

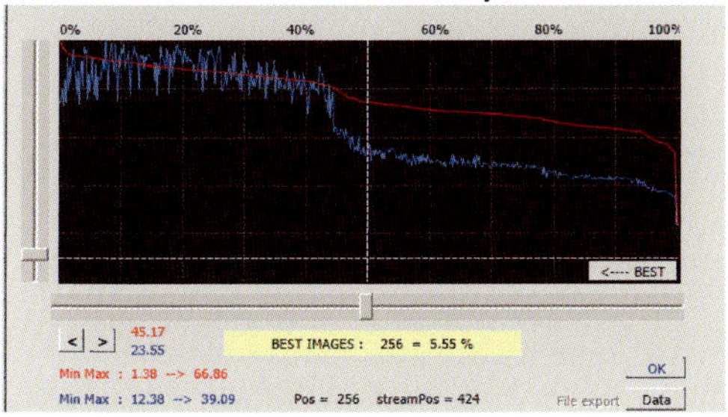

3. Analyse and select best images.

IMAGES TO STACK.
Either a **Full Stack** or a **Half stack** can be selected here. The % of frames to stack, or the number of frames.
The figures automatically populated into the settings can be accepted, or manually changed to include more or less images in the stack.

Play with these values to find the best settings for the data to produce the best stacked image.

4. Stacking Method.
Leave this on **Mean.**
Alignment Mode, select **Multi Points.**

Tile Size. The size of the alignment points can be manually changed, depending on the scale of the image. If stacking a full video size or Moon image, use a larger alignment point size. A smaller format sized video or ROI capture for planets require smaller alignment points.

I use size 48 for planet images and 72 for lunar images.

Experiment with this to find the best setting for the captured data.
4a. Click **Set**.
Several alignment points appear over the image.

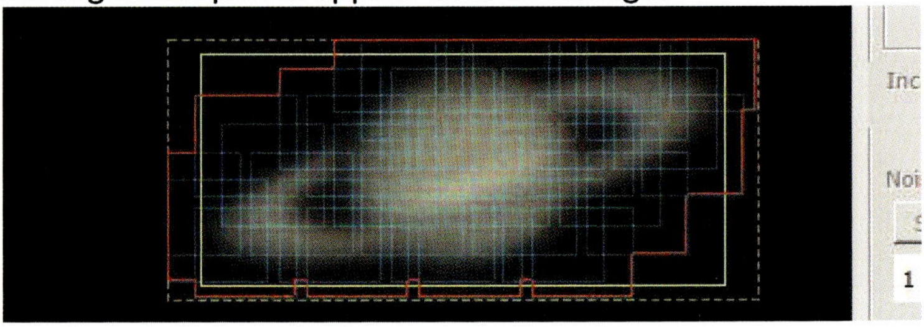

Under **Stacking,** select **As Video** to save the image in the same format and size as captured. Add some text to add into the name of the resulting stacking file, if required.

Tick **Align RGB Channels.**

Resize can also be used. A 150% change increases the size of the saved file. This may give sub-pixel interpolation to achieve a higher resolution, but this was dropped from the name of this option in the newer version. I have yet to confirm this is still the case.

5. Click **Stack.**
Once finished the stacked image is saved to the hard disk.
The images are stored in a sub-folder called **Aligned** which is located beneath the folder containing the original video file.

The stacked image opens within a smaller window.

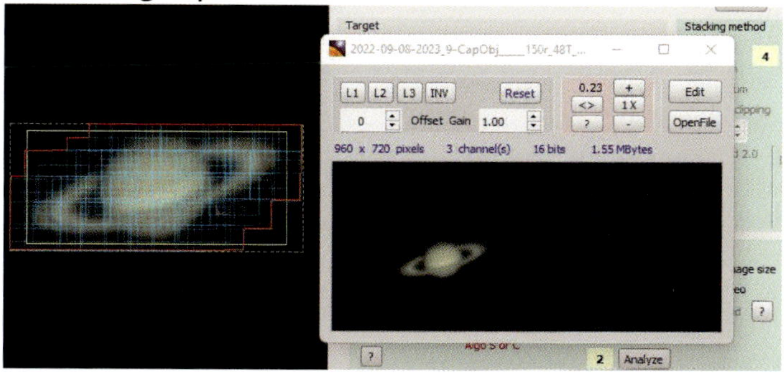

Click the **Edit** button, then click the **Yes** button on the **Analysed is opened!, Close It?** prompt.

The stacked image opens in the main AstroSurface window where it can be edited further.

Close the small Window as this is no longer required.

Post-Stacking Image Processing

Once the final image has been stacked, the tools within the software can be used to reveal the data captured by the camera and enhanced by the stacking process.

Both Registax or AstroSurface can be used for wavelet sharpening and colour balancing images. Both give great results, but each one can give different results depending on the quality of the data. AstroSurface currently has the edge for my images.

It is well worth going through both workflows in this guide to see what works best with the captured data.

Registax RGB Alignment.

Even when using an ADC to correct the image when capturing using a one-shot- colour camera, in many cases the red, green, and blue channel images may not always be aligned properly.
If **Align RGB Channels w**as used when stacking the image in AstroSurface, this step may not need to be performed.

Open the stacked image in Registax. If opening an image, the file type may need to be changed from within the drop-down menu to be able to see images rather than videos.

Click **Show Full Image**.

Under **Functions**, click on the **RGB Align** Button to open the tool.

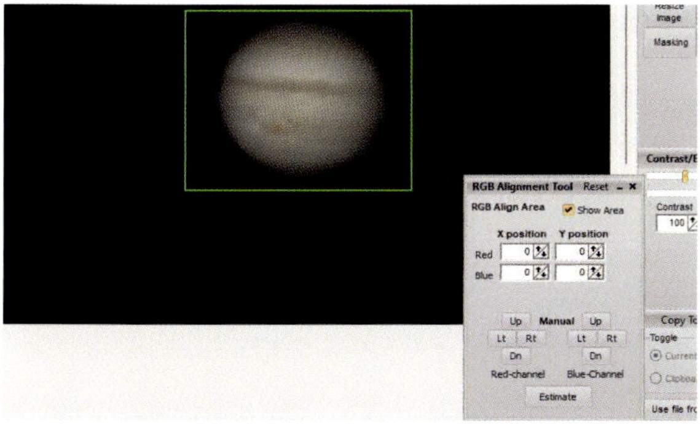

The adjustment can be performed manually, but the automatic alignment works extremely well.

Click the **Show Area** box, a very small green box appears on the image. Drag the corners of the green box to enlarge it to fit over the planet disk.

Click the **Estimate** button on the bottom of the RGB Align Tool. Nothing appears to be happening, and the software looks like it has stalled, but a progress bar has appeared at the bottom left of the Registax Window.

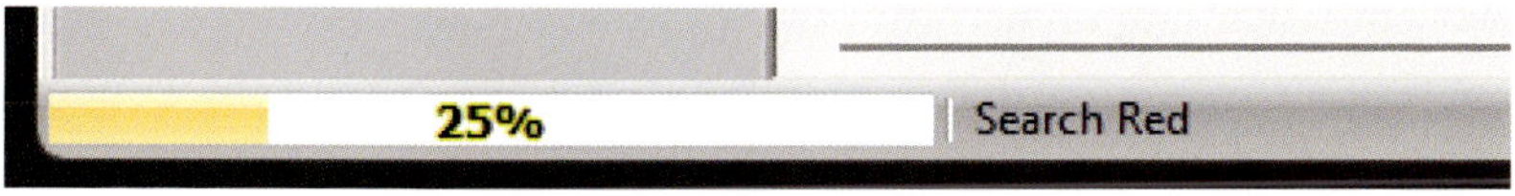

The progress bar displays ***Search Red***, then ***Search Blue***.

Once finished, the offset of the Red & Green Channels to the Green Channel are displayed within the Tool as shown below.

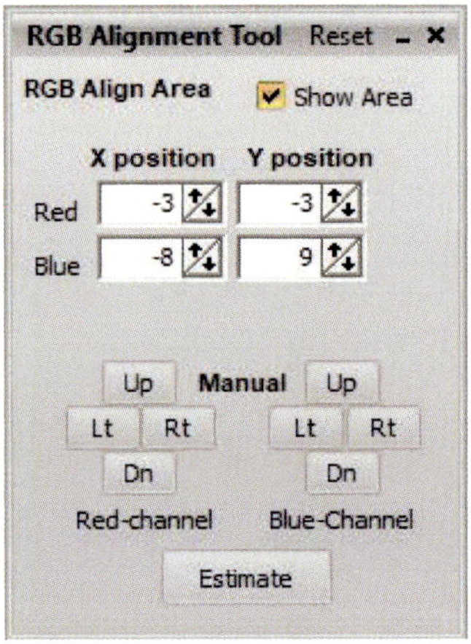

The position calculated is usually good enough to accept.

At the top of the Registax Window click **Do All** to apply to align the three colour channels across the whole image.

Close the RGB Alignment tool.

If needed, click the **Save image** button to save this image, changing the name of the file so that the original file isn't overwritten.

Registax Colour Balancing.

With some one-shot colour cameras, there is often a strong colour cast to stacked images. Lunar images often come out having a faint tinge of mauve or can appear too brown. Mars can also come out looking far too red and the other planets can have strange colour hues.
All these can be corrected using Registax.

Open the processed stacked image in Registax.

If opening an image, rather than a video, the file type in the drop-down menu may need to be changed to see images.

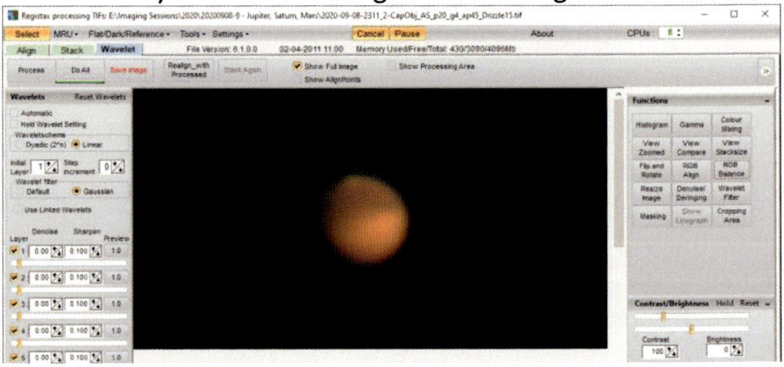

Click the **RGB Balance** Button.

A small Window pops up showing the three colour histograms.

The red, green and blue histograms are quite often not be aligned as shown in the image below.

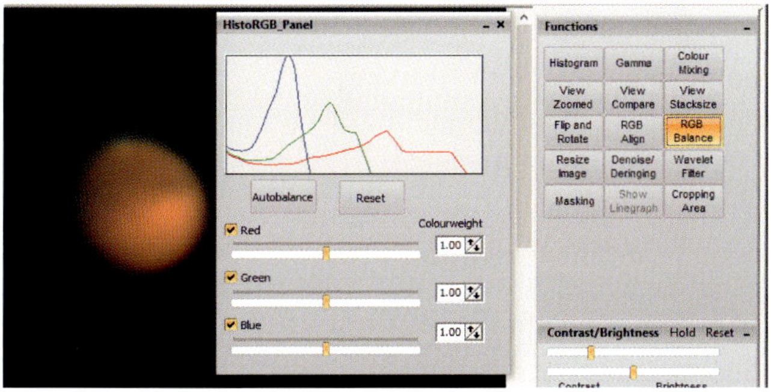

The red histogram is flatter and much further to the right. This makes the red channel of the image a lot brighter, hence the strong ruddy hue shown in the image.

Click the **Autobalance** Button.

This aligns the three colour histograms and removes any colour cast making the image look more natural.

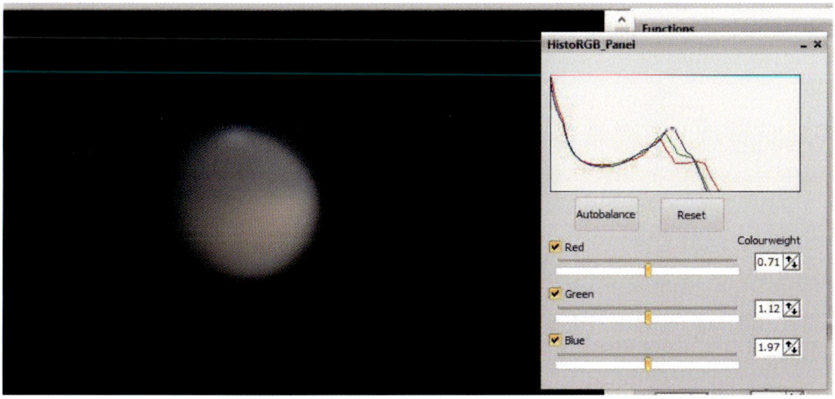

Don't worry if the colour looks a bit washed out at this stage, this be resolved later during post-processing.

Click the **Do All** Button. Click the **Save image** Button to save the image, using a different file name to avoid overwriting the original file.

Registax Wavelet Sharpening.

Open the stacked image in Registax or carry on after performing the RGB Alignment and Balance processes as described above.

The tool we are going to use for sharpening the image is Wavelets. These are visible on the left-hand side of the window when an image file is opened.

How do Wavelets work? I really don't have a clue. I do know that the different sliders work on different sizes of detail within the image. Everyone has a different opinion and use wavelets totally differently. If you look how other people use these, there is a lot of confusion on how they work and how best to adjust these to get the best results.

If the full image is not visible, to see what is going on in the full image, tick the **Show Full Image** box near the top of the window to fit the image to the window.

Everyone's data is different, so experiment to see what works best.

Like most photography the best results depend on the quality of the image that is being worked on. The better the image at the start of the process, the more detail can be extracted from it.

THERE IS A BIG WARNING HERE!
Overdoing Wavelets or any processing can introduce artefacts into an image, revealing features that just do not exist. So be warned.

It is easy to sharpen the image far too much. Less is usually best. Always try and keep the image as natural looking as possible when sharpening an image. This is true for any post-processing.

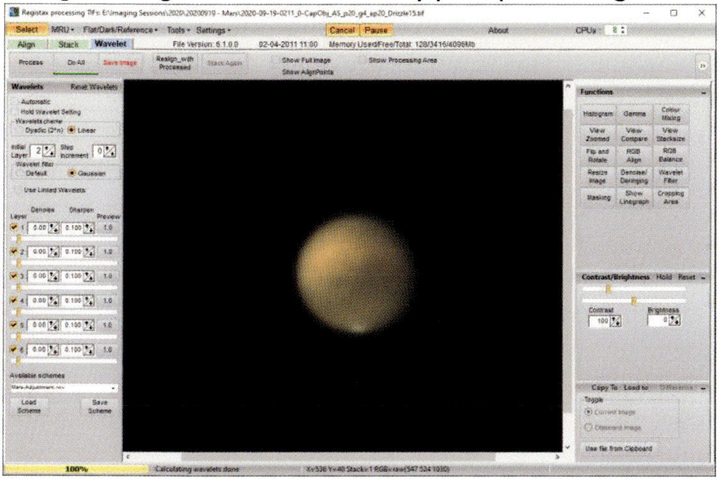

The first sharpening demonstration is leaving the **Waveletscheme** on **Linear**.

Set Wavelet Filter to **Gaussian.**
Move the lower Wavelet sliders from 6:3 further to the right than the ones above it as shown below. Below are the settings used to sharpen this Mars image taken on the 19th of September 2020.

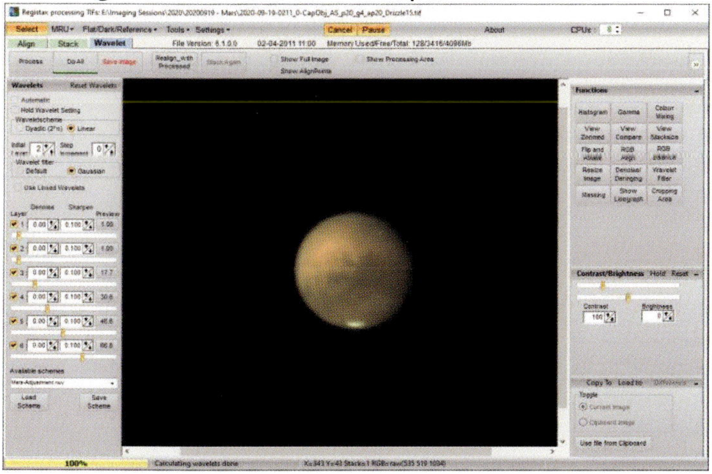

The centre of the image displays the amount of sharpening that has been applied to the image and details should now be more obvious.

When happy with the improvement, click the **Do All** button to apply the wavelet sharpening to the whole image.

When compared to the previous image it is obvious just how much more detail has suddenly popped into view.

Denoise and **Sharpen** adjustments can be moved up and down on the different wavelet levels. How effective these are at removing noise and sharpening depends on the quality of the stacked image.

To see how differently wavelets can be used, a very similar result is obtained by resetting the wavelets and then setting the **Wavelet filter** to **Default.**
Slide the 2:2 wavelet further to the right. Go down each level adjusting each one a little bit less than the one above it.
Increase **Initial Layer** value to 2.
This Initial Layer value multiplies how strongly wavelet sharpening is applied to the image. But this can often overdo the sharpening, introducing artefacts, so use it sparingly.

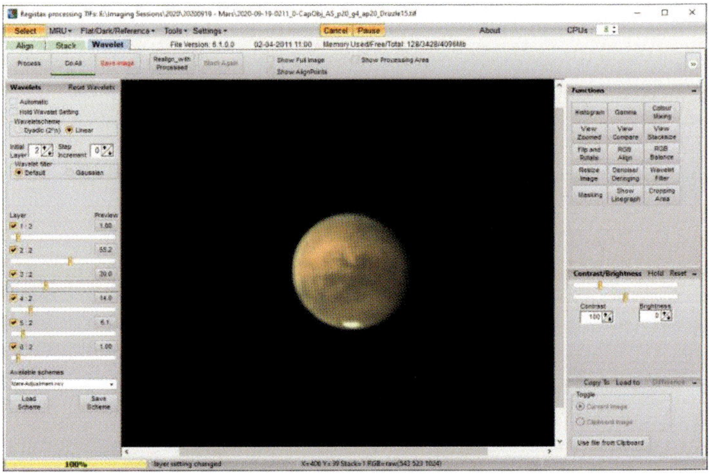

Different wavelet settings may be needed to bring out the best for different objects, stacked images and setups. Not all images need the same wavelet adjustments.

The key here is to use either of these two suggested settings as a starter and make further adjustments to the sliders to see which setting produces the best results for different images.

The key is to experiment, experiment and experiment even more, to find what setting really works for the images. Keep experimenting with this as the capture technique and processing changes.

There is also a tick box called **Hold Wavelets Setting**. Oncer ticked, the last settings are held. Any new image opened in Registax will have the same wavelet sharpening applied to it. This makes it very easy if wavelet sharpening many images from an evening out with the scope.

Once an adjustment is found that works well, this wavelet setting can be saved as a selectable scheme, using the **Save Scheme** Button.
These settings are now available from the **Available Schemes** drop-down menu next time Registax is used.

These saved settings can again be used as a starting point for each image, making further adjustments to the wavelets if necessary.
If the wavelets are sharpening way too much, start the process afresh by clicking the **Reset Wavelets** button to reset the wavelets.

Once happy with the sharpening shown in the preview square, click the **Do All** button.

Click the **Save Image** Button to save the image with a new file name to avoid overwriting the original image.

AstroSurface Sharpening.

These work in a similar way to wavelets in Registax, but gives a little bit more control over noise handling and gives a slightly better image.

Open the stacked (or previously colour corrected) image file in AstroSurface.

Under **ZOOM**, use the **-** & **+** buttons to zoom in or out on the image as required.

From the **Menu**, select **Filters > Wavelets-Deconvolution.**
The tool that opens has several adjustment sliders.

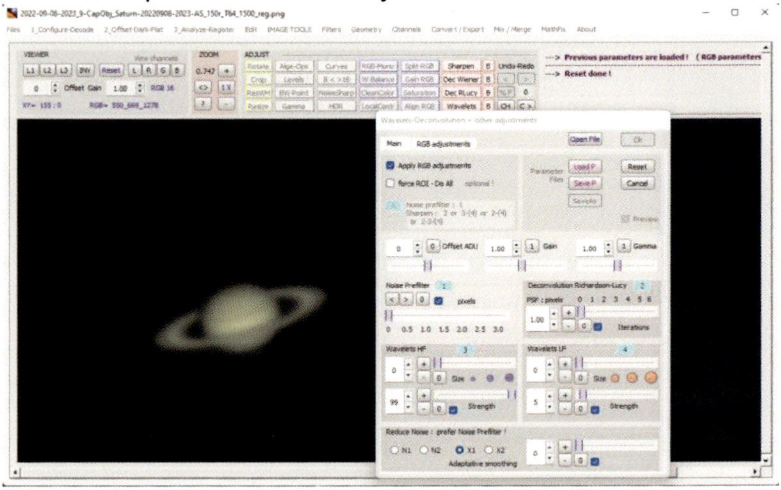

If processing large format images, it displays **(use ROI)** at the top of the Window. There is also a greyed out **Do All** Button below the **Cancel** button.

If these are visible, click onto the main image and draw a box using the mouse around the planet, or part of The Moon (ROI). This allows the software to show a preview within the box of that part of the image, while making the adjustments.

This helps to speed up the previewing process.

When working with smaller format images, if this option is not available there is no need to do this ROI selection.

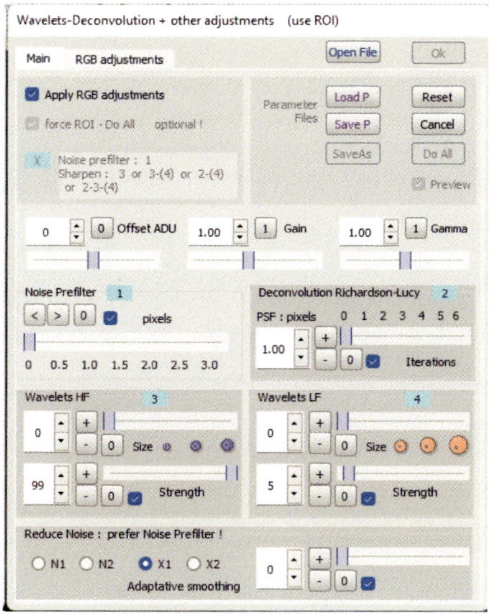

The software pops up a prompt to do this if needed.

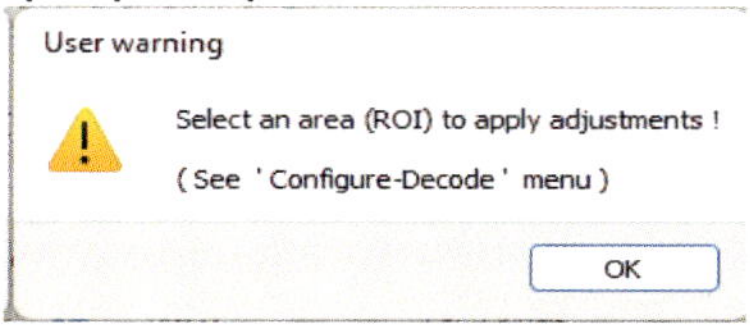

The main sliders used for sharpening are:
Wavelets HF, Wavelets LF, Noise Prefilter and Deconvolution RLucy.

Start the sharpening process by adjusting **(3) Wavelets HF Size**, and **Wavelets HF Strength.** (These sharpen smaller detail in the image). Increase HF until the image has been sharpened somewhat, and lower HF, increasing the sharpness until noise is just starting to become visible. It is a very delicate balance to try and get just right, without producing too much noise.
Adjust the **Wavelets HF Size** slider sparingly to the right as this can introduce a lot of noise into the sharpened image, especially if the original image is already particularly noisy. Move the **Wavelets HF Strength** to the left and try and obtain a nice balance between the two.

Inevitably, some noise starts to become visible in the image. Increase the value of **(1) Noise Prefilter** to remove this. Use this as sparingly as possible as it can blur detail.

When happy with these settings, adjust the **(4) Wavelets LF and HF** settings if needed. (This sharpens larger detail in the image).

If the image is nice and sharp, a small **(2) Deconvolution Richardson-Lucy** adjustment may also be applied.

Just making a few small adjustments to these filters can retrieve a huge wealth of detail out of an image.

The cloud belts and Cassini Division are now much more prominent by using the settings shown below.

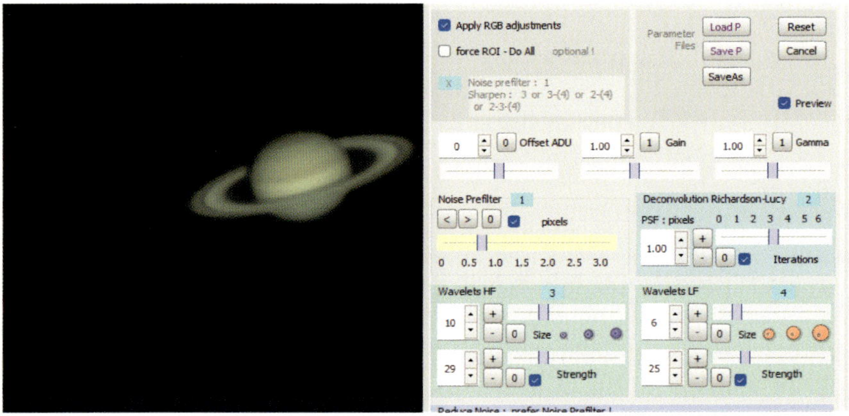

As with all sharpening processing, make sure that artefacts are not added into the image creating features that do not exist.

If not happy with the adjustments, the wavelets can be reset by pressing the **Reset** button to start afresh.

When happy with the result, if necessary, click **Do All.**

Then click **Ok.**

With some images, it may even be possible to apply one or more further less aggressive sharpening or noise reduction steps.

Save the image as a new file, by clicking from the menu, **Files > Save As: Image or ROI**, changing the name of the file to avoid over-writing the original image.

AstroSurface automatically remembers the settings of the filter. Next time the software is opened, and the tool is used, it applies the same filter settings to the image. Very useful if working on several stacked images. If needed these can be reset by pressing the **Reset** button.

AstroSurface White Balancing.

This can be done either before or after sharpening the image.
The stacked image of Saturn shown above has an unnatural yellow tinge to it. The White Balance Adjustment fixed this.

Open the stacked image file.
Menu. **Files > Open File SER-AVI RAW Digital**

On the menu under **Adjust**, click the button **W-Balance.**
The white balance is automatically adjusted, the colour now looks more natural.

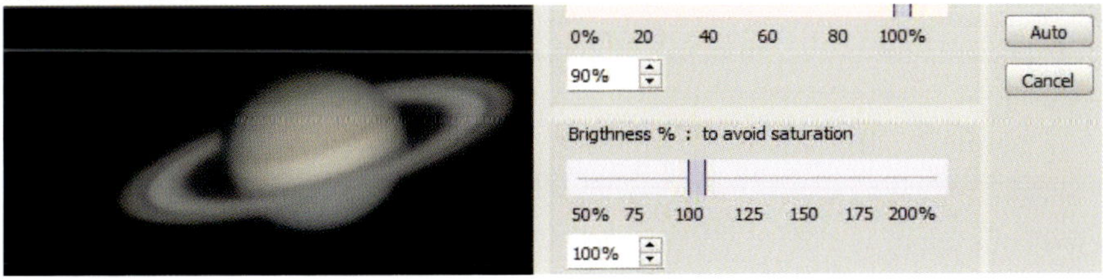

Click **Ok.**

If necessary, click menu, **Files > Save As Image or ROI** to save the image with a new file name to avoid overwriting the original stacked image.

Final Image Polishing.

Now that the main processing and sharpening of the stacked image is finished, there is some final polishing of the image to do to finish the job properly.

This can be with any image processing software. This guide shows how this can be done using both Photoshop and Affinity Photo.

Planet images have been used for many of these demonstrations, but most of these processing techniques can also be used on Moon and solar images.

These processes are only going to be described briefly, as I have astrophotography imaging guides for both Photoshop and Affinity Photo, which describe these and many more in much greater detail.

Post processing using Photoshop.

Rotating and cropping images.

Open the colour-balanced and sharpened stacked image in Photoshop. If the planet is tilted slightly, click on the **Crop** Tool from the left-hand toolbar.

Hover the mouse above a corner of the image frame until a curved arrow appears. Hold down the mouse button and move the curved arrow from side to side to adjust the angle at which the image is rotated.

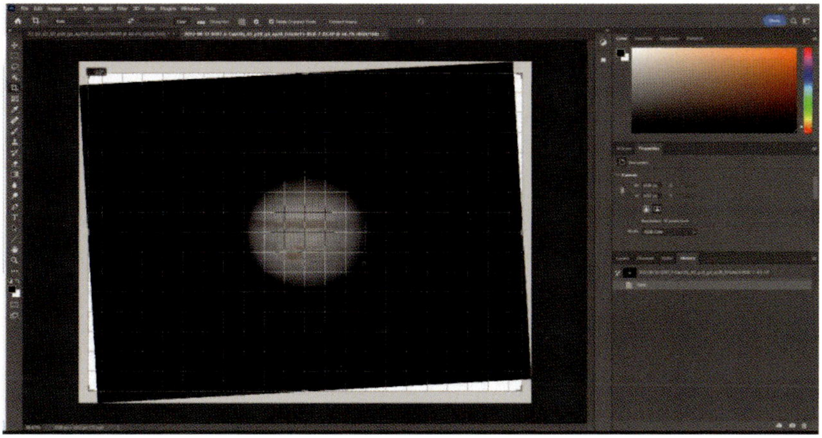

When the angle is correct, let go of the mouse button and double click inside the image. This crops out the edges and the planet should appear in the required orientation. Whether you put South at the top or not is down to you.

This tool can also be used to crop out any jagged edge problems often seen after the stacking process.

If needed the image can be saved with a new file name to avoid over-writing the original image. Menu: **File > Save As**

Brightness Adjustments.

Adjustments to brightness can be made using **Brightness / Contrast**, **Levels** and **Curves Adjustments**. These are available from the menu:
Image > Adjustments > Brightness / Contrast...
Image > Adjustments > Levels...
Image Adjustments > Curves...

These tools are self-explanatory. Brightness and contrast can be very rough adjustments, so best used sparingly. With this image I have only need to make a small sigmoid-shaped curves adjustment, which slightly brightens the image and increases the contrast.

Click **OK** to apply this change.

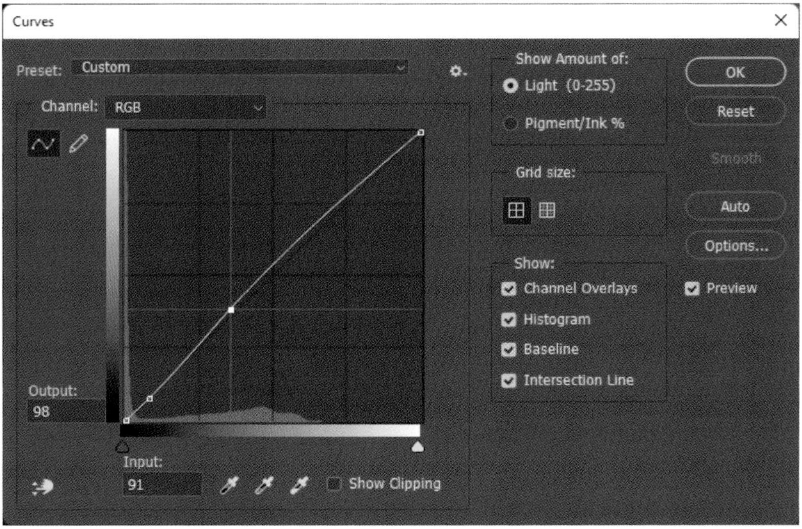

If needed, the image can be saved with a different file name, to avoid over-writing the original image. Menu: **File > Save As**

Sharpening The Image.

Another slight sharpening can be applied by using the Smart Sharpening tool. This is accessed from the menu.

Filter > Sharpen > Smart Sharpen.

Adjusting the **Amount** and **Radius** sliders starts to sharpen the image.

Slide the **Amount** adjustment further to the right than **Radius**, which gives the best result.

As before, be very careful that no unwanted artefacts are introduced into the image. Click **OK.**

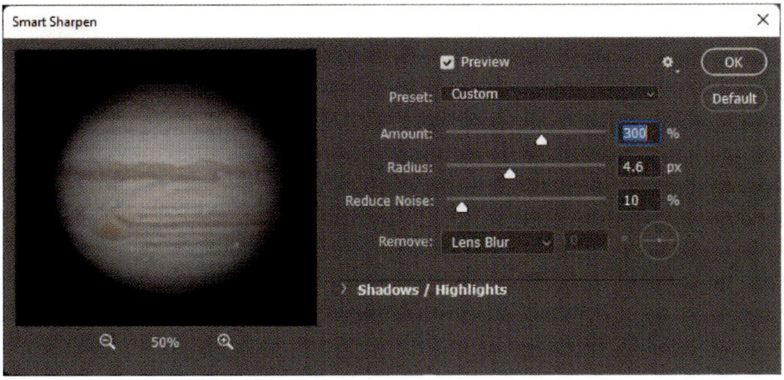

If needed, the image can be saved with a different file name to avoid over-writing the original image. Menu: **File > Save As**

Increasing Colour Saturation.

Now we need to bring back some of that colour we lost when we did the RGB alignment.
From the Menu, select **Image > Adjustments > Saturation**.

Slide the **Saturation** slider to the right to increase the saturation of the image revealing more colour.

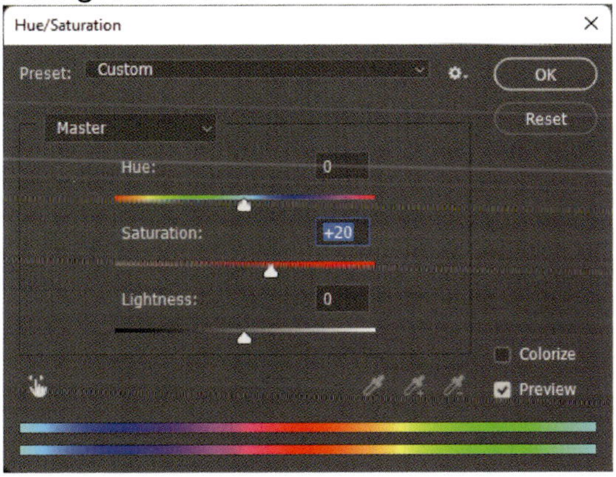

Don't increase saturation more than +20 at a time. Click **OK**.

This step can be repeated a few times to bring out more colour, if desired. But be careful not to overdo it to make the image garish and looking un-natural.

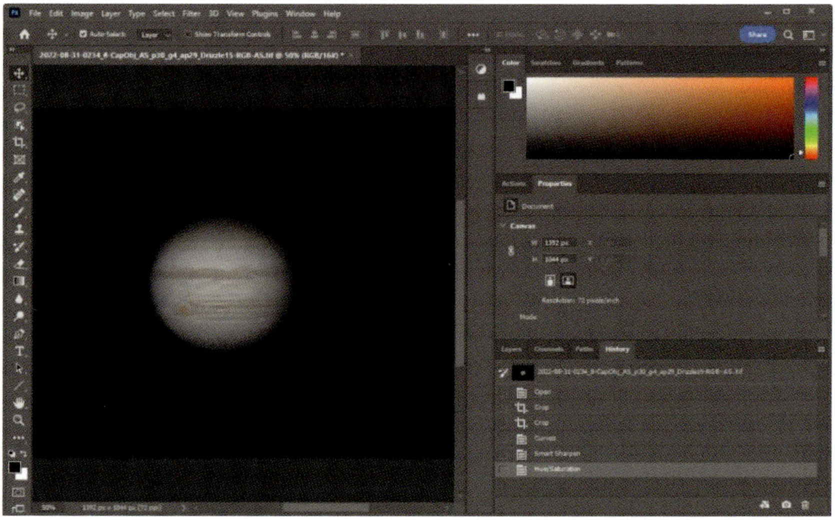

If needed, the image can be saved with a new file name, to avoid over-writing the original image. Menu: **File > Save As**

Revealing fainter detail.

In many lunar images, the surface nearer the terminator is darker than the rest of The Moon. This can often be lost in the stacked image as shown below. Using brightness or contrast adjustments can often make the brightest areas too bright and become over-exposed. We avoided this during the capturing process.

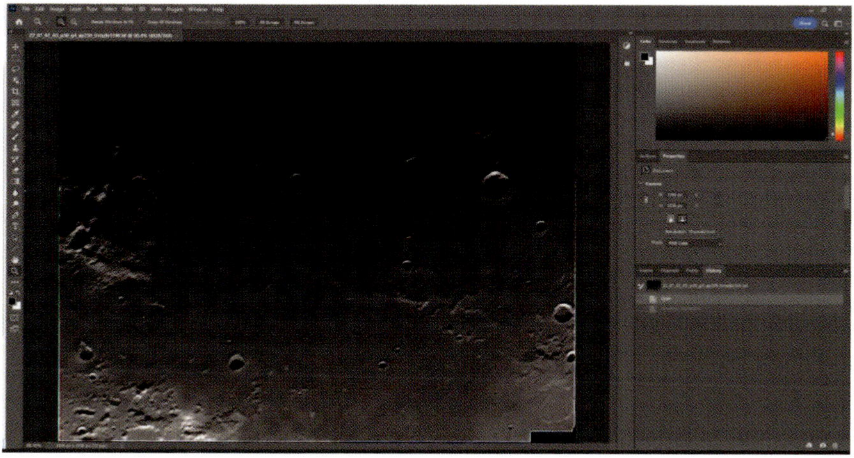

The best way to lift out the fainter features in Photoshop is to use the **Shadows / Highlights** Tool, accessed via the menu:

Image > Adjustments > Shadows/Highlights.

Slide the top slider, **Shadows Amount** to the right to increase the brightness of darker parts of the image.

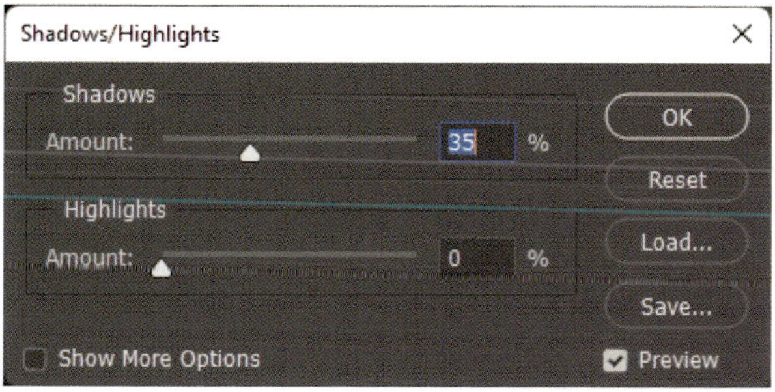

When satisfied with the adjustment, Click **OK.**

This adjustment has made the fainter parts of the image lying close to the terminator much brighter, revealing more features, without brightening and over-exposing the brightest parts of the image.

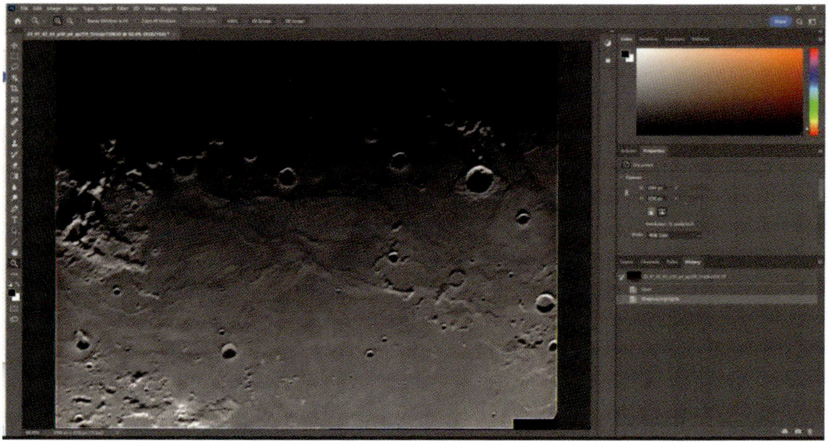

This step can be repeated several times if needed, but always make any adjustments in very small steps at a time.

Click menu: **File > Save As** to save the image as a new file to avoid over-writing the original image

Post Processing using Affinity Photo.

Open the colour-balanced and sharpened stacked image in Affinity Photo.

Rotating and cropping images.

If the planet is tilted slightly, click on the **Crop** Tool from the left-hand toolbar.

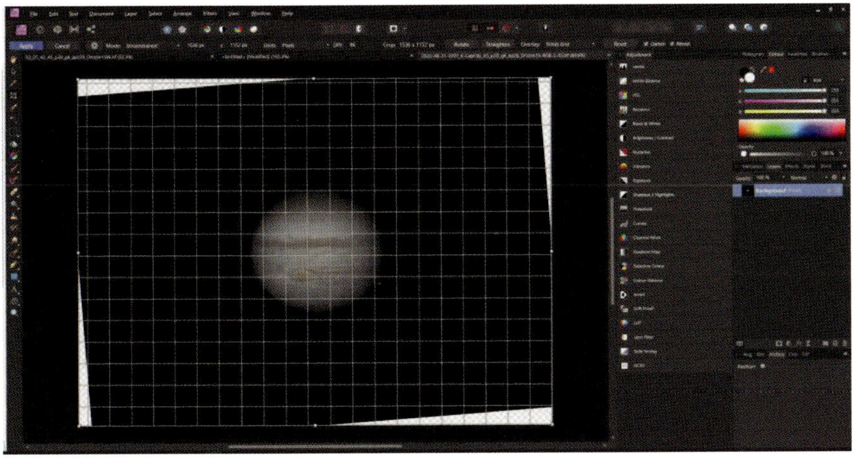

Hover the mouse alongside one of the corners of the grid, so a curved arrow appears. Hold down the mouse button and move the curved arrow around to adjust the angle at which the image is rotated. When the angle is correct, let go of the mouse button. Affinity Photo is non-destructive as it works, so will not automatically crop the edges.

Move the four corners of the crop tool inwards to get rid of the white areas appearing at the edges. **Double click** inside the image. This applies the crop so the planet is now in the required orientation.

Whether you put South at the top or not is down to you.

Brightness Adjustments.

Adjustments to brightness can be made using **Curves, Levels and Brightness/ Contrast Adjustment Levels**.

In this case only a small sigma adjustment using the **Curves Adjustment Tool** to slightly brighten the image and increase the contrast.

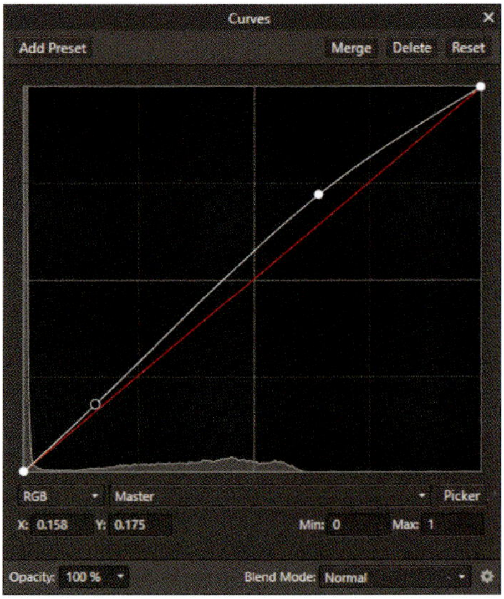

Click **Merge** to apply this to the image.

If needed, the image can be saved with a different file name to avoid over-writing the original image.
Menu: **File > Export >**

Sharpening The Image.

Another slight sharpening was achieved by applying a sharpening Live Filter Clarity layer. This is accessed from the menu.
Layer > Live Filter Layer > Sharpen > Clarity...

Slide the Strength slider to the right to sharpen the image.

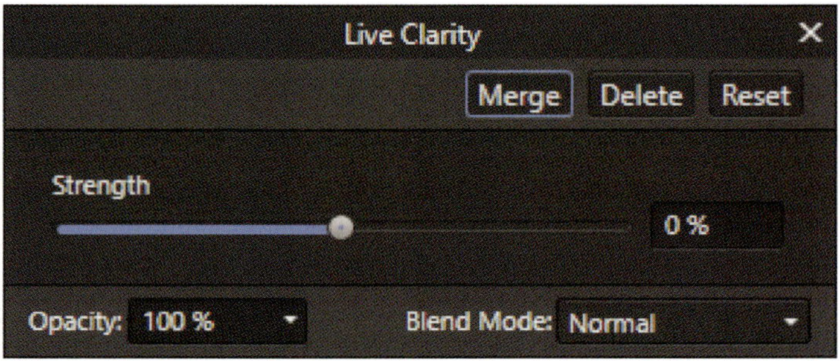

As before, be very careful that unwanted artefacts are not introduced into the image. Click **Merge** to apply this change to the image.

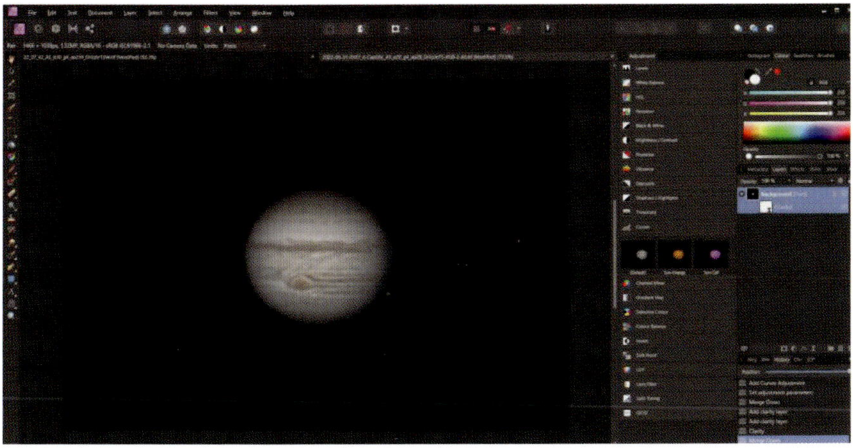

If needed, the image can be saved with a new file name to avoid over-writing the original image.
Menu: **File > Export >**

Increasing Colour Saturation.

Now is the time to bring back some of that colour we lost when we did the RGB alignment in Registax. This works well for the planets as well as revealing subtle colour differences in the regolith on the lunar surface.

This is done from the **Adjustments** Toolbar and the **Vibrance** Tool.

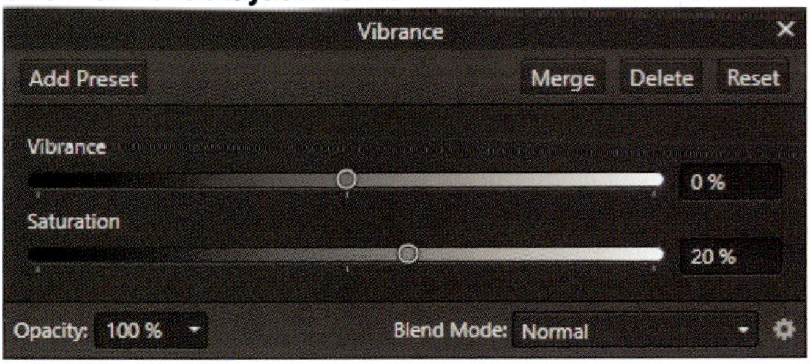

Slide the bottom **Saturation** slider to the right to increase the saturation of the image increasing the saturation of the colour.
Never slide this more than +20% at a time.
Click **Merge** to apply the change to the image.

This step can be repeated but use small steps at each stage and be careful not to overdo it to make the colours garish and looking un-natural.

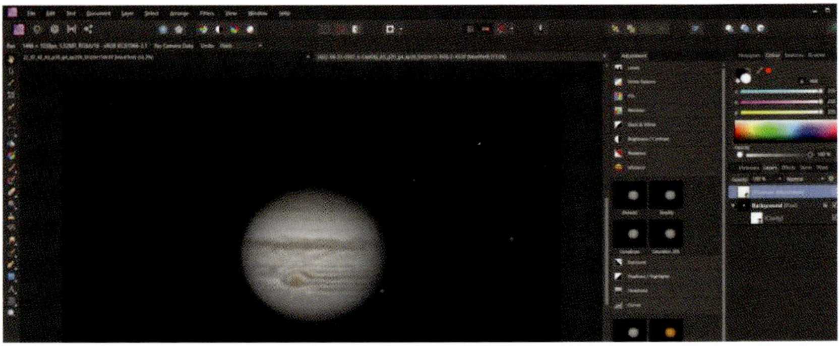

If needed, image can be saved with a different file name to avoid over-writing the original image. Menu: **File > Export >**

Revealing fainter detail.

In many lunar images, the surface when shooting near the terminator parts of the image can be a lot darker than the rest of The Moon.
This is often almost lost as shown in the image below.

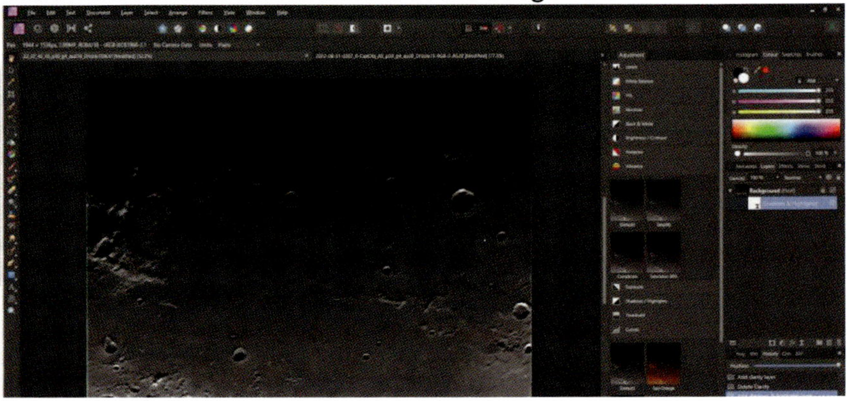

Using a brightness, contrast or curves adjustments can often make the bright areas far too bright so they become over-exposed. We already tried to avoid this during the capturing process.

The best way to lift out the fainter features in Affinity Photo is to use a Live Filter **Shadows / Highlights** Adjustment Layer.

This is accessed via the menu:
Layer > New Live Filter Layer > Shadows/Highlights.

Slide the top slider, **Shadows Strength** and the second slider **Shadows Range t**o the right to increase the brightness of darker parts of the image. I usually pull the top **Shadows Strength** slider further left than the **Shadows Range** as shown below to achieve the desired adjustment.

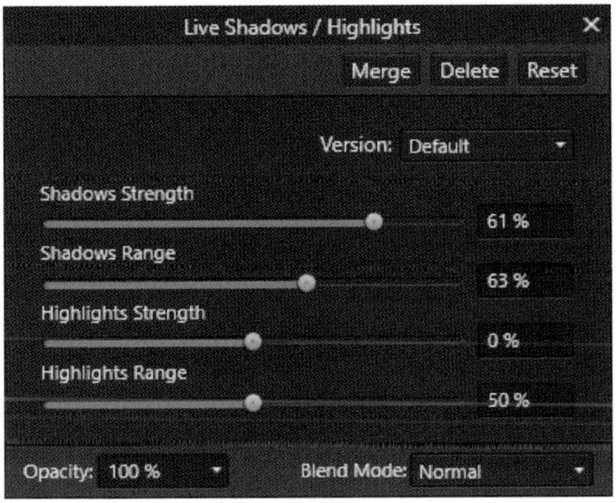

When satisfied with the adjustment, click **Merge** to apply this change to the image.

This adjustment has made the fainter parts of the image that lies close to the terminator a lot brighter, revealing those fainter features, without making much difference to the brightness of the brighter parts of the image.

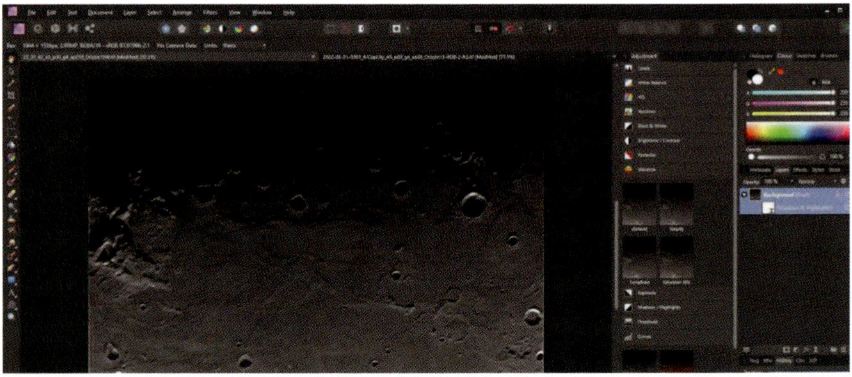

This step can be repeated several times if needed, but always make any adjustments in small steps each time to prevent overdoing it.

If needed, the image can be saved with a different file name to avoid over-writing the original image. Menu: **File > Export >**

All the images I have used for demonstration in this guide, as well as a few others, can be downloaded from my Web site to use these for practice:

www.star-gazing.co.uk/HiResImaging

I hope that my guide has helped you to get used to using the software and make great progress with your planetary and lunar imaging.

If it has, or you find any mistakes, please let me know.

Plus, if you have any hints and tips I can use for my next edition or post on YouTube or my Blog, also let me know.

E mail me at dave@star-gazing.co.uk

My image processing is constantly changing as I try out new techniques or find different software to achieve the intended results.
My capturing and processing workflow is as follows:

- Capture the AVI files I now use SharpCap (after using ASIStudio as I have ZWO ASI cameras).
  I will be looking at FireCapture very soon to see if that offers something any advantages.

- AstroSurface to Stack the Video. I used AutoStakkert! until very recently when researching and experimenting with software for this guide.

- Sharpen using AstroSurface Wavelets-Deconvolution Filter. As above, I used Registax for sharpening until very recently.

- Final polish and processing using Affinity Photo.

As I explore more and find different or easier ways to obtain better results, I am certain that my capturing and processing workflow will change going forward.

I will link any new workflows to the same Web page as the image downloads.
www.star-gazing.co.uk/HiResImaging

Other Useful Software / References

These software packages are not covered in this guide but are listed here for completeness.

FireCapture.
http://www.firecapture.de
This is free software. Donations are welcome if you find the software useful. It has a handy image stabilisation mode that could work well, but I have not experimented with this yet.

PIPP – Planetary Imaging PreProcessor.
https://sites.google.com/site/astropipp/
Free software is used to process video to align the individual images in a new stabilised video prior to stacking.

WinJupos.
http://jupos.org/gh/download.htm
Free software. Enables de-rotation of images for stacking.

SER Player
https://sites.google.com/site/astropipp/ser-player
Open source software for playing and viewing SER files.

VirtualDub.
https://www.virtualdub.org
Free utility to edit videos and extract individual frames.

Planetary System Stacker.
https://github.com/Rolf-Hempel/PlanetarySystemStacker
Another useful video stacking software package.

SiriL.
https://siril.org/
Free software for stacking and enhancing videos and pictures from various file formats.

Look out for my other astrophotography guides which are available for purchase from my Web site:
http://www.star-gazing.co.uk/WebPage/guides

Photoshop Astrophotography Image Processing.
Affinity Photo Astrophotography Image Processing.
Imaging the Moon.
Deep Sky Stacker: Deep Sky Objects and Comet Images.
Solar Webcam Imaging.

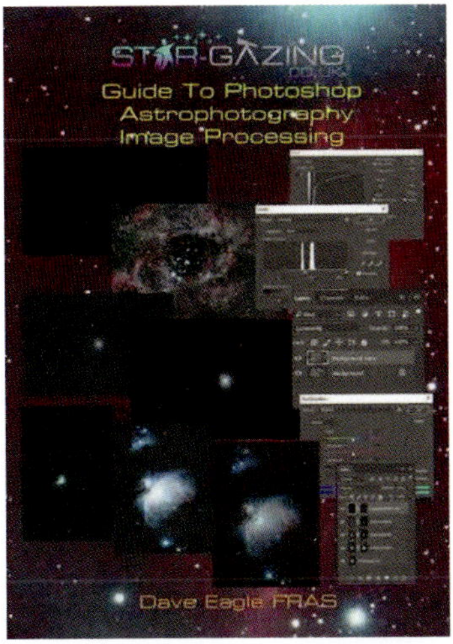

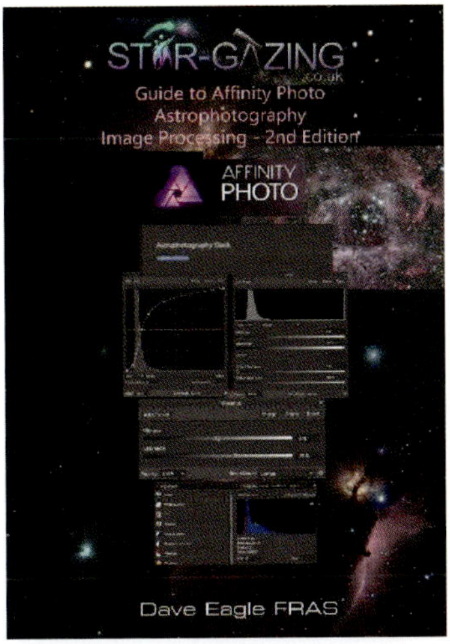

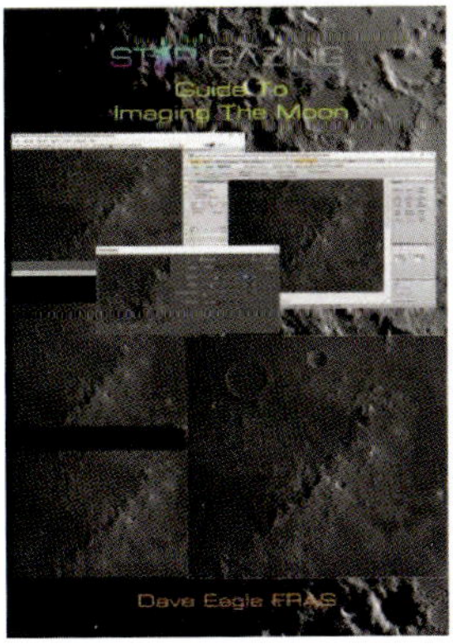

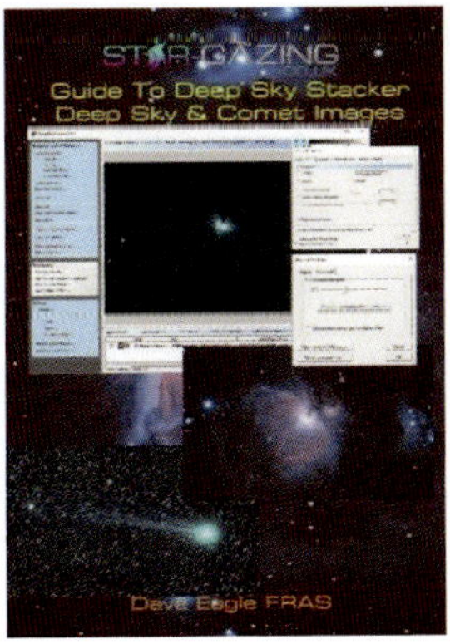

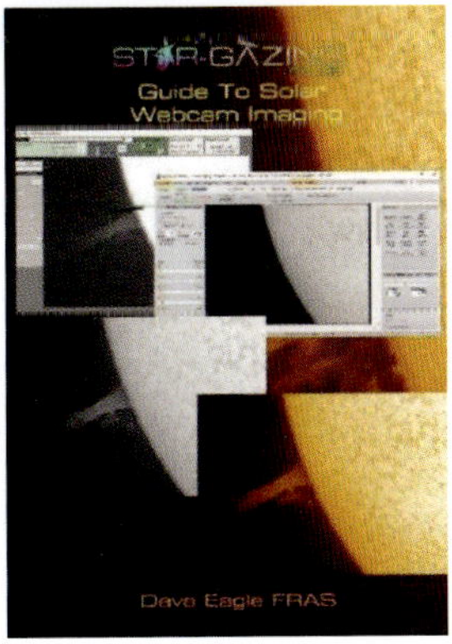

Workshops:
My hands-on astronomy and astrophotography workshops are available for booking from my Web site:
www.star-gazing.co.uk/Workshops.html

121 Tuition:
I also do one to one tuition, either in person or via Zoom.
Just give me a shout if you'd like to book a session.
www.star-gazing.co.uk/121

Find or follow me online:
Web: www.star-gazing.co.uk
Facebook: https://www.facebook.com/Eagleseye45
Twitter: https://twitter.com/Dave_StarGeezer
Flickr: https://www.flickr.com/eagleseyeonthesky
YouTube: http://www.youtube.com/DaveEagle-Star-Gazing

STAR-GAZING .co.uk

Guide to High Resolution Lunar and Planet Imaging

Dave Eagle FRAS

www.star-gazing.co.uk